# FARMYARD
# & FOUR OTHER PLAYS

# FARMYARD
# & FOUR OTHER PLAYS

*By Franz Xaver Kroetz*

Urizen Books New York

For American and Canadian performing rights, contact Mr. Kurt Bernheim, 575 Madison Avenue, N.Y., N.Y. 10022. Tel: 212/753-5320

*Wunschkonzert* © 1973 Suhrkamp Verlag, Frankfurt am Main. Translation © 1975 by Peter Sander, Suhrkamp Verlag, Frankfurt am Main. © 1976 by Urizen Books, Inc., New York.

*Stallerhof* © 1971 Suhrkamp Verlag, Frankfurt am Main. Translation © 1976 by Michael Roloff and Jack Gelber.

*Michis Blut* © 1971 Suhrkamp Verlag, Frankfurt am Main. Translation © 1976 by Michael Roloff and Denise Gordon.

*Männersache* © 1971 Suhrkamp Verlag, Frankfurt am Main. Translation © 1976 by Michael Roloff and Carl Weber.

*Ein Mann, ein Wörterbuch* © 1973 Suhrkamp Verlag, Frankfurt am Main. Translation © 1976 by Michael Roloff and Carl Weber.

ISBN 0-916354-12-1
13-X

**Library of Congress Cataloging in Publication Data**

Kroetz, Franz Xaver, 1946-
   Farmyard, and other plays.

   I.  Title.
PT2671.R59A25        832'.9'14       76-47569
ISBN 0-916354-12-1
ISBN 0-916354-13-X pbk.

# Contents

# Introduction

## by Richard Gilman

"I am a theater person who mistrusts nothing as much as the theater," Franz Xaver Kroetz told an interviewer a few years ago. This assertion brought the young German playwright into some very good company. At one time or another, Büchner, Strindberg, Chekov, Pirandello, and Brecht expressed sentiments of the same order; Ionesco has revealed his abiding disappointment in the life he witnessed on the stage, and Kroetz's own brilliant contemporary Peter Handke has made disbelief in the ordinary practices of the theater a ruling element of his dramaturgy. It would seem as though the drama, to a much greater degree than the other arts, requires of its geniuses an at least preliminary attitude of skepticism, contempt, and even revulsion.

The reason for this isn't hard to find. Along with opera, its related form, drama is the bourgeois art par excellence, the one most tempted toward the reinforcement of existing cultural values and so, by extension, of social and moral values, too. The matter is more subtle than ideology or any form of direct persuasion; what theater does, when it is operating to deaden consciousness, to act as a consoling and confirming ritual, is to reproduce an *expected* life, to present models of experience (or wishes, dreams) which the audience has already had and about which it has already come to conclusions. Again, it isn't a question of obvious comfort or palliation; "painful" plays, drama about suffering of one kind or another, may also be bourgeois—in the sense of being complacent, essentially optimistic, unable to imagine life otherwise than as it has been known—as long as the depicted suffering fits easily into preexisting molds. There is a *place* for suffering in any well-rounded bourgeois education.

In a prefatory note to his short play *Heimarbeit (Homeworker)* Kroetz has composed a terse manifesto for all his work, a statement that reveals the particular basis of his mistrust of the conventional theater at the same time as it sets out the ground on which his distinctive imaginative sympathies rest and from which they seek their objectifications. "I wanted," he writes, "to break through an unrealistic theatrical convention: garrulity. The most important 'action' of my characters is their silence; and this is because their speech doesn't function properly. They have no good will. Their problems lie so far back and are so advanced that they are no longer able to express them in words."

A drama built on silences. A theater of the inarticulate. Such is the ironic achievement of this playwright who is scarcely thirty and has already established himself as a wholly unexpected and astonishing force in his native theater and is likely to do so soon in theatrical consciousness everywhere.

Set until very recently (the change is greatly significant, and I shall take it up later) in the urban lower-class and poor farming milieus of his Bavarian childhood and youth, Kroetz's plays offer what would seem to be a chamber of horrors of violence and scatology. A spinster returns from her factory job one evening, goes through her precise rituals of lonely domesticity, and then calmly, gravely kills herself. A script calls for a man to masturbate and defecate on stage (of course in production the actions are simulated or shown indirectly) and for a girl to foul her pants from fear. There are abortions or attempted ones in several plays. A dog is shot in another; a man and a woman use each other as targets in a deadly game with a rifle; an infant is murdered; illegitimacy, adultery, and perverse sexual acts run through all the texts. Everything is dumb, animal-like, without any dimension of "mind."

Knowing only this much, one might properly conclude that Kroetz represents a retrogression, a movement back to a grim and fatally circumscribed realistic mode. Or, on a coarser level of response, such as that which greeted the opening of *Homeworker* in Munich in 1971, when Catholic organizations among others picketed the theater and rotten eggs were thrown at its facade, one might see no overriding artistic purpose in the display of such "tasteless" and malodorous material. Yet there seems to me no question that Kroetz is among the most remarkable new writers for the stage of the last fifteen or twenty years, and by new I mean in sensibility, vision, and technical procedure. To begin to know how this may be so, despite the appearance of datedness or crude sensationalism which any summary of his plots and dramatic incidents would present, we have to return to the note to *Homeworker* quoted before.

Kroetz's great quiet originality lies in the fact of his having broken through, as the note tells us he wished to, a theatrical convention—an iron principle would not be too strong a term for it—that has held dominion over the stage throughout almost all its history and in nearly every one of its sectors, transcending questions of style and theme and coming almost to represent dramatic reality itself.

"Garrulity," he calls it, affixing a pejorative connotation to what we have always thought of simply as speech, dramatic utterance, oral expression on the stage. So unquestioned has been the existence of speech, dialogue, as the central agency of dramatic values, the chief means by which consciousness is shaped in the theater, that to accuse it of being "unrealistic," misleading, a convention, and not the precise heart of the matter is to seem to be quarreling with the very nature of the theater and of drama as a form. Yet we ought to know from our own lives, even if we lacked a theater to bring it formally to our attention, that garrulity—the overabundance of speech, its runaway mode—is designed to hide truth even more than to reveal it, and to mask the hiding: "methinks he doth protest too much" is a response to garrulity having been found out. To speak too much serves to cover up with words the holes in our existence, the spaces of unmeaning or of meaning too painful or dangerous to be permitted lineaments.

It is these spaces, these holes that Kroetz's plays can be said to offer as their dramatic vision or actuality. A paradox? A contradiction in terms? How does a vision arise from emptiness or substance from absence? Well, so nurtured are we on a belief in language as the most direct instrument of meaning in any literary work (and drama, while a peculiar form of literature, an enacted one, we might say, is nevertheless literary) that we find it dizzying to try to imagine how its absence or, more accurately in regard to Kroetz's plays, its maimed presence might be more significant and evocative than its fulness. The richer the language, the greater the work, we think; Shakespeare is the criterion and the apex. And this is all very well, and true, except for the moment—the repeated moments in the history of the theater—

when garrulity takes over, when there is too much being said.

A starting-point for an understanding of what this "too much," this excess of utterance, might be, as Kroetz conceives it, lies in another remark to an interviewer that "my figures are incapable of seeing through their situation because they have been robbed of their capacity to articulate." The word "robbed" alerts us to the political dimension of Kroetz's theater, but for the moment the thing to see is that the statement could function by inversion as the most concise possible history of traditional "high" drama, for that might be defined precisely as the *seeing through* of situations, replicas or analogues of those experienced in life, on the stage.

To do this one needs speech, which is to say the power of naming the condition one is in (if not directly then by verbal structures that create it metaphorically; the most "eloquent" plays do it just that way), of making distinctions both within it and between it and other states, and therefore of making it, in theory at least, *useful*: instructive, purgative in Aristotle's sense, eye-opening in Brecht's, in every case part of the formal stock of human awareness. And, Kroetz is saying, until now, throughout the long reign of the theater as a cultured activity, such a power has been the possession only of the privileged, in an economic sense, surely, but also in a wider one. It has belonged to the more or less articulate, by definition. Drama in this view has consequently offered us, in a way that transcends subject or idea, a world in which characters, deputies for the rest of us, own from the start the means of making their situations known, of expressing them, so that whatever else a play may be it is essentially a process of bringing this knowledge into the light.

What is more, the knowledge is itself privileged, the self-awareness of those human beings in the guise of stage characters whose social existence, and so whose existential space, is wide enough to permit thinking about, giving names to and so truly experiencing—although not of course necessarily "solving"—their predicaments: Lear's knowledge that he has lived not wisely but too well, Norah's that she must leave her husband in order to find out what she is. If such knowledge is continually being corrupted and turned into bravado by garrulity (in the commerical theater garrulity is all there is) which papers over the chasms and so hides reality at the same time as it seems to proclaim it, the principle remains undisturbed that it is only through language that the attempt to know can be made, and the belief is firm that drama is one of our chief means of organizing this expressive intent.

Now, this doesn't in any way mean that there have been no poor or stultified, "inarticulate" characters in drama. The point is that where they exist they have not been at the center of the work and have been surrounded by characters who can speak and so carry the burden of verbal meaning, or else, as in Tolstoy's *Power of Darkness*, O'Neill's *Hairy Ape,* or Gorky's *The Lower Depths*, they have been given a passionate "popular" utterance of their own and so are made articulate after all. (The one great exception might seem to be Büchner's Woyzeck, yet even this unprecedented figure of the oppressed and victimized possesses speech, broken, tormented, mad if you will, but greatly evocative speech nevertheless.) On a more debased esthetic plane the poor and outcast have usually been given an articulateness that is the product of romantic invention, the fake urban lyricism of Odets or the cracker-barrel loquacity of plays like *Tobacco Road*. In any case, the condition of being truly unable to utter one's reality has never been a central element of any play, has never, one can almost say, been a subject.

In place, then, of characters whose command of language is their precondition for being characters and who talk so that we may "appreciate" them (appreciate: to judge with heightened perception and understanding) and so presumably be made more conscious, Kroetz has created figures whose speech does nothing either to bring forward ideas or perspectives on their condition or to cover it up, and in fact only "expresses" it negatively by its injured or inadequate quality. They seem to speak only because people do, struggling to find some connection between words and the internal conditions or facts of the world which make up their situations; they speak, one feels, because not to speak at all would be the conclusive evidence of their despair.

In the opening scene of *Michi's Blood,* a scene which with characteristically quiet irony Kroetz calls *Table Conversation*, a man and a woman, lovers or at least sexual intimates, exchange these words:

# I TABLE CONVERSATION

MARY: Since we've only got this room you can go to the john.

KARL: It's cold in there.

MARY: Ya can't just take everything lyin' down.

KARL: Yeah.

MARY: Cause you're a filthy pig.

KARL: That's what you are; what's that make me?

MARY: You're crazy.

MARY: You're horny, but you can't get it together.

KARL: That's what you are; what's that make me?—I don't give a shit.

MARY: Don't eat if it don't taste. Think I'd stop ya?

KARL: Not you, cause I wouldn't ask.

MARY: Don't bother eatin' if it don't taste.

KARL: Tastes okay.

MARY: Ya don't love me no more. That's it.

KARL: If ya know it anyway.

MARY: That doesn't help none.

KARL: How's a body gonna eat in peace?

MARY: Am I botherin' you?

KARL: Not you for sure, cause I don't give a shit about ya!

MARY: It used to be different.

KARL: That's all over.

MARY: When ya need someone and he notices, then he don't know how ta appreciate that.—Want me ta leave ya alone?

KARL: I want my peace and quiet.

MARY: No one's sayin' nothin'.

KARL: I've had it.

MARY: Leave it, then we got somethin' for dinner.

KARL: A bitch if there ever was one. It makes me puke when I see it.

MARY: Go ahead, think I'd stop ya? No one asks me whether I like it or not.

KARL: Just you call me a shithead.

MARY: Shithead. Pig, you're a filthy pig. I'm gonna sic the cops on ya.

They'll put ya where ya belong. And I worked my heart out for someone like that. That guy got no gratitude at all.

KARL: I'd do it again right now.

MARY: Why doncha?

KARL: Yeah.—Stop bawling if ya don't git what I say.

MARY: I understand ya all right.

KARL: Cause ya are dumb.

MARY: Better dumb than a pig.

KARL: I jist don't like it no more.

MARY: No one's asked whether they like it or not.

KARL: I've had enough.

MARY: No one's like ya. You're crazy; plain as day.

KARL: Ya can't do nothin' for it.

MARY: Yeah.

KARL: Shut up and keep out of things.

MARY: I've got my rights, too.

KARL: Ya got nothin'.

MARY: You're a drunk and a lush.

KARL: Yeah.

MARY: Antisocial ya are.

KARL: An old bag ya are.

MARY: A bum.

KARL: A slut.

MARY: I'm not.

KARL: Sure ya are.

Later, after the woman has revealed her pregnancy, the man gives her a crude abortion. A scene called *Finding the Truth* goes as follows, in its entirety:

MARY: Can I tell ya somethin'?

KARL: Why not?

MARY: I've got a pain.

KARL: Then pull yourself together. You'll manage; just don't think about it.

MARY: Yeah. One should never lose hope.

KARL: So what d'ya want?

MARY: I just don't know no more.

KARL: Probably somethin' stupid anyhow.

MARY: Yeah. Cause I forgot.

KARL: Always gotta add your two bits.

MARY: Why?

KARL: There.

MARY: I'm human too.

KARL: Christ. That's somethin'.

MARY: I'm tryin' to be serious.

KARL: Ya think I'm not? Ya think I'm any different?

MARY: I know that about you.

Now the painfulness of these exchanges rises both from their substance, naturally, but even more from their relation to the play's events or, more accurately, the expected significance of those events, their "values." In the first scene the quarreling lovers (if we can call them that; their relationship mocks all the classic, lyrical attributes of the word) stumble verbally round one another, exchanging blows of sad, depleted forcefulness, blows without point, delivered in the dark. The clichés, the repetitions of banalities, the bromides all testify to the stricken nature of their speech, not so much its lack of expressiveness—that is obvious—as the entire absence of originality, the queer and terrifying sense it gives of not having been created by them but of having instead passed through them, as it were. It is as though their language has been come upon, *picked up*, scavenged from the grey stretches of a mechanical culture.

In the second scene the pathos of this derivative, radically inappropriate speech is still deeper. We know from what has gone before that the woman is anguished over the abortion, or rather we have to intuit it since she is wholly unable to express it in terms we would think appropriate. The man, for his part, is embarrassed, frightened, bellicose; but once again these emotions and attitudes have no appropriate style, no diction we can accept as directly constituting the experience, the way traditional drama has always organized its effects. The clichés and fragmented responses, the sad aphoristic wisdom (One should never lose hope! Kroetz's plays are full of such sayings in the mouth of victims), move to fill the space between feeling and event, but the gap remains intact. And it is from this abyss that there rises the extraordinary sense in the spectator of being present at a sort of fatal accident, a crack-up at the edge of truth. "I'm human too," the woman says. We know she is, but the sorrowfulness of the remark is that she has been injured past the capacity to demonstrate it.

If the damaged speech of Kroetz's characters is their most striking departure from conventional stage figures, it doesn't mean that the physical in his work is any less original. If anything, the physical action in these plays is more mysterious and disturbing than the verbal, not so much in its substance as in the ways it is disposed. Where the connection between speech and physical action in traditional drama might be said to be that of comment and reciprocity—an "acting" out of the verbal, a "speaking-out" of the material—in Kroetz's plays this relationship is ruptured; the two orders of expressiveness never fuse, never offer direct perspectives on one another. Nothing is done as a *consequence* of something having been said, or the other way round.

The clue to this strange new relationship of speech and act lies in Kroetz's remark about the most important "action" of his characters being their silence. For these silences, the gaps within or the truncation of their speech, make for an almost unbearable tension on the stage, a pressure of the unsaid—of the unable to be said—that weighs upon every movement or gesture, and all potential ones, and infuses them with a quality of extreme nakedness, radical isolation. Bereft of the "cultural" covering in which dramatic actions are ordinarily sheathed, the matrix of articulated ideas, attitudes, perceptions, comment, and so on, these physical events take place, so to speak, inexplicably, like eruptions from the darkness, pure, horrifying acts of discrete and seemingly motiveless violence.

The most extreme of them, the murders, rapes, assaults that fill his plays, come at a point when the felt inadequacy of their language, the frustration they cannot name (and, still worse, cannot even imagine with a name, since that would be to possess some part of the language whose lack is their very condition) bring his characters to pass over the boundaries of the "civilized." It is as though the tension created by their inarticulateness, the profound occlusion of consciousness in them, can only give way to the "relief" of brutal motions, to a catharsis in which nothing is purged but something infinitely painful is, at least, attested to.

This deeply subtle relationship of speech and gesture in Kroetz's plays, this atmosphere made up so largely of the implicit and unannounced, makes their strange power and effectiveness unusually difficult to convey through brief quotation or the description of single actions. Still, a scene such as the following one from *Farmyard* offers us a narrow way into the depleted, stricken world his imagination has come upon. A middle-aged farmhand has taken the young, retarded daughter of his employer to a country fair. They take a ride on the "ghost-train" and when they emerge from the tunnel the girl is evidently in distress:

# ACT II

## Scene I

*(A small county fair, early afternoon, a dead time.* BEPPI *and* SEPP. BEPPI *completely fascinated.* SEPP *slightly drunk.)*

SEPP:    You gotta wish?

BEPPI:    *(doesn't react)*

SEPP:    Want to ride the merry-go-round? *(It's a ghost train)* You afraid? Look at those big dolls.

BEPPI:    *(afraid, fascinated)*

SEPP:    Come, let's take a ride.

    *(takes her by the hand to the box office)*

SEPP:    One adult and one child.

    *(they take the ghost train)*

    *(return)*

BEPPI:    *(disturbed)*

SEPP:    It was nice wasn't it?

| BEPPI: | (uncertain) |
|---|---|
| SEPP: | What's the matter? |
| BEPPI: | (walks stiffly) |
| SEPP: | Something hurting you? |
| BEPPI: | (denies it) |
| SEPP: | You dirtied your pants. You did. Come on now. Were you scared? |
| BEPPI: | (completely confused) |
| SEPP: | Or was it the soda pop? Come on we'll clean you up. (They go behind a tent or away from the crowd. Here, wipe yourself with these leaves. |
| | (She cleans herself; diarrhea runs down her legs.) |
| SEPP: | You shit in your pants. Here let me. (He cleans her up.) Take off your pants, you can't run around like that. (BEPPI cleans herself with his help.) Wipe yourself with this. Here let me. (He takes his handkerchief and wipes her with it.) It's all right again. (pause) Come here. |
| | (He takes her and deflowers her.) |

The scene is of course harsh, unsettling, "embarrassing" to witness. But what strikes one throughout is the entire inability of the girl to speak about or to the situation (although she is slightly retarded, she is in no sense a mute) and the man's extreme matter-of-factness in his speech to her, a matter-of-factness that is greatly at odds with what the theatrical spectator is conditioned to expect and that prepares the way for the brutal abruptness with which he takes the girl's virginity.

The cold, terse stage direction in which this is indicated is an exemplary instance of Kroetz's methods (if that is the right word; I would prefer to say his angle of vision): the absence of either preparation or aftermath, the refusal of comment, the sudden, isolated, terrifying act of violence. An actor or director might wish, out of obedience to notions of proper "theatricality," to insert some stage business between the last line of the dialogue and the rape, but it is precisely Kroetz's genius to cut through such dramatic integument in order to present the most naked, unmediated, and, to the degree that this is possible, *unestheticized* gesture and image. One result of this is an extraordinary compactness; since nothing is elaborated or filled in, the play, like others of his, moves with a sort of implacable speed, leaving no time or space for the audience to account for and so diminish its strange power.

This cold, grave quality of Kroetz's plays, their eschewal of judgment, argument, and authorial bias, the absence in them of any trace of tendentiousness, of "color" and emotional solicitation of a traditional kind, and, finally, their extreme simplicity of incident and iconography are what so sharply distinguish them from the species of drama we have historically called "naturalistic." Apart from a mutual repudiation of fantasy and the elevation to the status of characters of previously excluded beings—the poor, the outcast—his plays have almost nothing in common with the dramas of classic naturalism, Zola's, say, or Hauptmann's. Above all, they do not share traditional naturalism's dream of a quasi-scientific imperium, its enslavement by what Delacroix called "the fetish for accuracy that most people mistake for truth."

By the same token, Kroetz's work protects itself through its internal dispositions, its sense of mysterious fatality and unassuageable pain, from the charge of sensationalism, of an intention simply to shock, although the accusation continues to be made. His plays are as far from *Tobacco Road* or any newer mode of sexual "frankness" on the stage as it is possible to be; they may seem to be dealing with some of the same materials and ambiances, but the difference is of the order of that between C. S. Forester's and Joseph Conrad's treatment of the sea, an absolute difference of size, mind, and moral imagination.

In fact, the disturbance Kroetz has caused, as well as the welcome given to him by more discerning minds, goes far beyond the immediate physical data of his plays to the broader implications of his style and the esthetic and cultural significances they radiate. The truth is that his breaking of moral and social taboos, his unhygienic displays and feral anecdotes, are in the service of a far more subversive vision than they mount up to in themselves; his presence speaks of a wider imaginative change in German theater—so often a force for change in the universal stage—than one could discover by a recounting of his "stories."

*Homeworker* was one among a number of unsettling new plays that appeared in Germany at the end of the sixties and the begin-

ning of the seventies and were the work of a wholly new genera-
tion of German (and in some cases Austrian) dramatists of whom
Kroetz is likely the most gifted and surely the most original. Men
born during or just after the war, the group includes Martin Sperr,
Wolfgang Bauer, and Rainer W. Fassbinder (who is better known
in the United States for his films); and while they differ widely
among themselves in matters of style and sensibility, they also
share certain deep affinities. They are all to one degree or another
left-oriented in politics; they employ vernacular speech in prefer-
ence to any sort of literary language; they have set themselves
against the use of the stage as a source of what they consider de-
bilitating illusion; and, most significant for their creative morale
and imaginative independence, they have been freed—by acts of
the will as well as by chronology—from the previous era of devas-
tated German consciousness.

This group of writers, to whom for the sake only of a con-
venient identity we might give the collective name of "new
realists," constitutes, I think, the most vigorous and in some ways
innovative movement in the theater since the renaissance of the
British stage that was carried out fifteen or twenty years ago in the
early plays of Osborne, Pinter, and Arden. The more pertinent
comparison, though, is to the appearance in Paris in the early fif-
ties of what we have come to call—at the cost of as much confu-
sion as the term New Realists is likely to cause—"absurd" drama, the revelatory, unexampled plays of Beckett, Ionesco, and
others. For what these young German playwrights have been doing, Kroetz most forcefully among them, is the same kind of
life-giving work as that of their antipodal predecessors in France:
the extrication of the theater from its own assumptions, from re-
ceived wisdom and settled notions of what drama is and what it
may do.

These writers make up, that is to say, an avant-garde, but one
which neither proclaims itself as one nor bears the obvious distin-
guishing marks of such an enterprise. There ought to be nothing
surprising in this; it is outsiders who usually give avant-gardes
their name, and, in regard to the signs by which they will be
known, it is one of the grand subtleties of culture that the truly
newest forms generally owe their animating principles to achieve-
ments reached in the past and often appear to us precisely as old,

although with a strange, unaccountable light flickering over their surfaces, the light of something newly seen.

In the case of these new German playwrights the debt is to the old and for the most part underground tradition of the *Volkstücke*, or "folk play," which was not, as its name suggests, a work of naive authorship, rising from some memorializing or celebratory impulse among simple people, but the highly conscious creation of sophisticated writers for the theater. Its chief characteristics are that it concerns itself with the lives of common people and that it is written either in dialect or in one or another kind of colloquial language, in opposition to the *Hoch* or "high" *Deutsch* in which the overwhelming majority of German plays have always been composed.

The form was introduced in Vienna in the early eighteenth century by a writer named Josef Anton Stranitzky, and was carried to a full development by the nineteenth-century Austrians Johann Nestroy and Ferdinand Raimund. Then after a long period of neglect it was revived in the twenties and thirties of this century, chiefly by the gifted German writer Ödon Von Horvath (whose neglect here—he has scarcely been translated—is a minor cultural mystery). Von Horvath, who died young in 1939, wrote plays whose characters were mainly petty clerks, small shopkeepers, housemaids, hustlers, grifters and the like, the marginal, tamped down people of modern urban life, plays which were free of the didactic moralizing that had marred the work of Nestroy and Raimund.

Von Horvath's influence on Kroetz and his fellow neorealists is clear and acknowledged by them, but their most direct and powerful predecessor, as they unreservedly avow, is a writer with a strange, painful history who figures in only the most marginal accounts of twentieth-century German literature and is entirely unknown here.

Marieluise Fleisser, who died in 1973 at seventy-one, wrote plays (as well as novels and stories) about the most oppressed of characters, the socially insulted and injured, employing a coarse, ragged vernacular for their speech and exhibiting them in an atmosphere of spiritual desolation. Brecht took an interest in her work, and although their ideas and style were far apart, they clearly seemed to have learned something from each other. The victim of psychic disorders and domestic turbulence, at various

*Farmyard & Other Plays*

times of censorship and, almost throughout her career, of public indifference, she was "rediscovered" in the late sixties by Kroetz, Fassbinder, and others and has since enjoyed a certain vogue. Before her death she met Kroetz, who has carried her vision and techniques to a much more extreme point. She called him "the dearest of her sons" and went on to say, with an understatement characteristic of both him and herself, that "he cares about the others."

This caring, which is clearly so much more than abstract concern for the victims of social and economic injustice, has, as I have tried to point out, entered Kroetz's work without fanfare or any kind of declaratory impulse whatsoever. And it is just this quality of austere detachment, the placing before us, without comment or the least grain of theatrical seductiveness, of imaginative *evidence* which makes up a stringent, self-validating dramatic whole, that helps lift these plays out of what we might call their "local" status, their possible existence as case histories.

For however specific his characters' milieus may be, however identifiable they are according to our typologies of social organization, dramatically they exist as deputies (Kroetz's own word for them) for all of us. They have particularly grave afflictions and employ their own blind means of combatting them, but they stand the way we do—the articulate, readers, writers, audiences—in the face of the chasm between language and truth, self-awareness and fate, closer to the extreme edge, of course, but not constituting a different species. They speak, or struggle to speak, for us all.

Still, the judgment I have just offered is essentially an esthetic one, and the theater is notoriously a place where esthetic reality has a hard time making itself known. Our compulsion to construct moral hierarchies among human beings has been given particular encouragement in the theater—heroes and villains, the absolved and the condemned; it is one of the subtle bourgeois conventions of the stage at which Chekhov, as he tells us, used to "swear fiercely." And though the phenomenon is scarcely confined to the theater, the medium is especially disposed toward the corruption of a "virtue" such as pity into a sense of superiority or, at best, into a mode of proper, civilized, ineffectual response; you pity the sufferer, who remains in place for your pity to exercise itself upon.

In the light of these things the crisis of conscience that overtook Kroetz several years ago is far from surprising. A mistruster of the theater, a man of strong leftward leanings, he had seen behind the suffering of his characters an "expropriation," a "stealing" of their language, as he called it. He had seen politically, in other words, and because, as he thought, "my pieces keep producing primarily apolitical pity," he took certain steps to try to correct that. In 1973 he joined the West German Communist Party, and though he has claimed that he has experienced no pressure, that he has been encouraged to write in the "same way as before," the fact is that his writing has changed drastically.

The first indication of this was his having written (a few months before his formal entrance into the Party, but when he was well along toward the decision) an unabashedly "agitprop" work called *Münchner Kindl*, a play about the housing situation in Munich and the growing concentration of land and capital into the hands of a few oligarchic families, which contains a direct call to tenants and the exploited generally to join the Communist Party. His most recent play, *Das Nest* (The Nest), carries him further along the retreat from his earlier stance of pure untendentious vision as well as, thematically, from his icy tales of the dispossessed. The drama is about ecology and the conflict between values and power, its characters are of the middle class and, entirely unlike Kroetz's earlier figures, have no difficulty at all in "expressing" themselves; to be articulate about their problems, or rather about social questions, is what makes them fit to function in a traditional drama.

But perhaps the most disturbing evidence of Kroetz's change is in his having rewritten an earlier work in order to make it conform more closely to his present belief and attitude. This play, originally called *Men's Business* (an ironic title conveying Kroetz's erstwhile deep sense of women as even greater victims than men), ended with a shocking, unbearably painful yet superbly revelatory scene in which a couple play a "game" with a rifle and so allow their mute antagonisms and unfulfilment to find their fatal expression. Kroetz has retitled the work *A Man, A Dictionary*, which comes from a nearly untranslatable folk saying, and, much more radically, has eliminated the culminating scene and given the play a more or less "happy" ending. (The two versions are printed in this volume.)

*Farmyard & Other Plays*

Kroetz is young, and he cares. We have to sympathize with him in his dilemma and refrain from condemning in the name of "art" what seems to be a movement toward an obvious and unresonant facticity. Some time ago he spoke poignantly of what lay behind his changed position. "My pieces," he said, "are oriented on very Christian conceptions: they appeal primarily to empathy, to love among people, to insight, to understanding, to giving something up of one's free will, to improving something of one's free will; they are touching, they do not agitate, offer no solutions, and therefore lend themselves particularly well to being absorbed as a kind of warm breath."

If he fails to see the truly remarkable dimensions of his earlier accomplishment, its revolutionary shift in consciousness and powerful, exemplary beauty, he is surely justified in his suspicions of the fate of any kind of imagination in the world of institutionalized culture. Like other writers before him (Tolstoy comes immediately to mind), he is caught between his social awareness and concern and his *prédilection d'artiste*. Whether or not his new mode of didactic dramatic invention will be permanent is beyond even our speculation. Meanwhile the earlier plays remain, testing us, challenging our habits, harsh, unaccommodating; and heartbreaking.

# Translator's Note

The translation of Kroetz's *Farmyard* and *Michi's Blood* presented unusual difficulties in that they are written in Bavarian dialect. At first I thought the translation required a casting of the plays into an indigenous American dialect, say, the speech of the mountain people in Tennessee and Kentucky. But after seeing performances of *Farmyard* in London and at Yale University, and of *Michi's Blood* also at Yale University, I concluded that the plays retain their innate power despite the absence of an identifiable local dialect, that some form of crippled ordinary speech would suffice. As they are printed here, the two plays incorporate this rehearsal and performance experience. Wherever else they may be performed, the director and the actors will want to draw on their own experiences.

*Men's Business* and its revised version, *A Man, A Dictionary* are written in a less obtrusive dialect and therefore required less adaptation in that direction. Karl Weber and I feel that the original and the revised version can be combined to mutual advantage, particularly so as to retain the pessimistic ending. Franz Xaver Kroetz disagreed with this view, and so we are publishing both versions simultaneously.

—M.R.

# Request Concert

*Translated by Peter Sander*

This play presents a situation which I have often noted in police reports. Suicide is, in many cases, unbelievably tidy. The preparations for suicide do not violate the victim's mundane, everyday activities; and the act itself is performed with the same love of order, as neatly, as uprightly, and as silently desperate as the life which provoked it.

This says a great deal about one's life today; its unfulfilled expectations, its hopeless prospects, its little daydreams. It documents one's inability to shake loose the slavery of production; it can show that one's life and one's passing from life resemble that of beasts of burden.

Like animals these people communicate their desperate situations by remaining mute, which implies a stern measure of order, of resignation, or an unquestioning acceptance of "things as they are," of exploitation, and of repression to the point of infirmity and collapse.

If the explosive force resulting from this exploitation and repression were not self-directed, that is, against the exploited and repressed themselves, we would have a revolutionary situation. Instead we have many cases of suicide and murder which only serve a positive purpose in that the perpetrators, having summoned up enough power and courage to throw their own lives into the balance, deliver themselves up unto the jurisdiction of their natural enemies. Thereby they involuntarily cleanse the society they condemn. So, in becoming the condemned themselves they disappear into prisons or into graves, which amount to the same thing.

This is the only way that the inhuman order in which we live and must continue to live can be maintained.

## The Setting

A naturalistic set of a rented apartment. As is usual with old subdivided houses of this sort, one can imagine how the other apartments are set up and rented out. One gets to the toilet via a long hallway.

The room itself stands in contrast to what one imagines the other apartments might look like. It is exceptionally clean, conventionally petit-bourgeois, neat, and arranged with hominess, love, and warmth.

The spectator must be able to visualize that in a sea of cheerless, uninhabitable tenement houses, someone has with great love, effort, and taste created a place that rises above its environment.

Naturally, on the other hand, an industrial and worker's atmosphere pervades everything.

## Character Description
Fräulein Rasch is between 40 and 45 years old, black hair, about five feet tall. She still has a good figure. Only her legs are rather thick, as if she suffered from water retention.

Her complexion is dark, not the sort of tan one aspires to and finds attractive, but rather what one might call dirty. Fräulein Rasch makes a rather plain, average impression, so that her apparent unattractiveness, although not totally hidden, is somewhat softened.

Her choice of dress proves her to be a woman of discretion. Her clothes are conservative and of good quality. One senses that she pays a great deal for them. Fräulein Rasch is employed in a stationery factory, where her job is to tend to the envelopes.

At any rate, we find ourselves in a small city, and Fräulein Rasch's monthly take-home pay is 615.50 DM (about $205.00).

Because of her involuntary virginity, or what amounts to the same thing, her involuntary sexual abstinence—after one early, short, and painfully sad love affair—Fräulein Rasch is particularly susceptible to romance. Therefore she spends as freely as her income allows, which may be seen in her furnishings, her wardrobe, and her personal grooming.

## About The Length of This Play
Naturally the play must not irritate the audience, but it must provide insights for them, about the emptiness of Fräulein Rasch's life. Care must be taken that the actual activities in the play are not drawn out so as to become tedious and aggravating. When the informative content of an ac-

tivity is exhausted and it only repeats itself, it should be broken off, even if it violates the form of the play, namely that stage time is equivalent to real time. I would guess that the play would not last any longer than a good hour.

What can be shown

- "plain, average, unattractive woman"
- a worker
- cold-water flat
- apartment-house exterior (mail) + hallway

Not showable

- what she does at work
- her salary
- her involuntary virginity.

## Part One

On a normal workday Fräulein Rasch comes home at about 6:30 P.M. after work and after her shopping. She enters the apartment house, checks her mail, finds only an advertisement, takes it, goes to her door, unlocks it, and steps in. She lays her shopping bag with her groceries and a newspaper on the table, sets her purse on a chair, hangs the advertisement on the sideboard, and locks the door.

She takes off her coat, pulls it over a hanger, and hangs it on a hook on the door. She spies a spot on the back of the coat. Then she crosses to the window, touches the radiator to feel if it is hot yet. Carefully she pulls the curtain aside and opens the window a crack.

She discovers some dirt on the window sill, takes a rag off the pipe under the sink, and cleans off the whole sill. She puts the rag back and begins to unpack the groceries and put them away in the refrigerator, the sideboard, and the breadbox. Then she hangs her shopping net on a nail next to the stove.

She takes off her high heels, puts them in the closet, and slips on her house-shoes that stand next to the closet.

She takes off the jacket of her attractively tailored suit and hangs it in the closet on a hanger. From the closet she removes an old cardigan and puts it on.

Then she walks over to the mirror next to the stove by the sink and removes her earrings, her necklace, and her ring. She lays this costume jewelry in a dish on her chest of drawers, returns to the mirror, looks at herself for a long time, and fixes her hairdo with a comb and brush.

She pays particularly close attention to a pimple that has gotten worse since the morning; and after she has washed her hands she rubs the spot with cream.

She heats some water on the gas stove for washing dishes even though there are not many to wash. It is a cold water flat, and she uses her large sink for all her washing, cleaning it thoroughly after each use.

She goes to the TV set in the corner and turns it on. Then, sitting at the table, she takes the advertisement from the sideboard and opens it up. She reads it carefully and sets it aside. From her purse on the chair she pulls out a pack of cigarettes—Lord Extra—and a lighter. She lights one. Meanwhile the TV has warmed up and she watches it. It is a commercial or some other pre-primetime program. Slowly and thoughtfully she smokes her cigarette. Then she puts it in the ashtray on the sideboard, goes to the chest of drawers and takes up the TV program lying on top of it. She returns to the table, lays the program out on it, gets the ashtray with the lit cigarette from the sideboard, takes her purse off the chair and puts it at the end of the sideboard.

She sits down again, leafs through the TV program to see what is on this evening. She takes a last puff of her cigarette and carefully snuffs it out.

She gets up, goes to the stove and turns the gas off, returns to the table, stands there, and leafs through the TV to the radio section. She studies it and finally crosses to the TV set and turns it off. She looks at her wrist watch and takes it off, laying it next to the other jewelry. She takes the program, folds it up, and puts it back in its place.

(Note: In Bavaria, on Wednesday nights at 7:15 there is a radio program called "As You Wish" with Fred Rauch, which is especially popular when it presents popular music or light classical selections—sometimes it alternates popular, light classical, operetta, and opera. At any rate, one gathers that a dull television program is less interesting to her than this popular radio show.)

She ties on an apron, lets some cold water run into the sink, and pours the hot water in. She takes a pile of dishes from her small meal and washes them quickly and efficiently.

Finally she dries them and sets them away in the sideboard. She puts a plate and a silverware setting on the table for her supper. She drains the water out of the sink and cleans it up carefully. Then she washes her hands and rubs lotion on them. She takes several things out of the refrigerator and puts them on the table. Because she can get a hot meal at work, she eats only a cold snack for supper.

# Part Two

She goes to the radio and turns it on. Then she walks over to the table and sits down. She butters a slice of bread. With a wave of her finger she indicates that she has forgotten something.

She stands up again and takes a bottle of fruit juice out of the refrigerator. She gets a glass from the sideboard, pours some juice into it, and fills it up with water. She puts the glass on the table with the other things and sets the bottle back in the refrigerator. Then she sits down and begins to eat.

She eats thoughtfully; lovingly she prepares each slice of bread. She listens to the request concert attentively and laughs whenever Fred Rauch tells a joke. She daintily swallows small sips of juice.

After supper she meticulously puts the things together, wraps up the butter and the sausage, puts the lids back on the jars. Then she lights a cigarette and smokes it all without doing anything else.

She gets up, clears the table, and puts everything back in its original place. She puts the dishes *(a plate, a fork, and a knife)* on the sink counter.

She leaves the room and goes to the toilet. It takes quite a while until she can wipe herself. This, too, is done as pedantically and as hygienically as one can imagine. She pulls the chain and cleans out the bowl with the brush standing next to the toilet. She opens the lavatory window a crack.

She returns to her room and washes her hands, thoroughly, crosses to the radio, and adjusts the tuning because some static has drifted into the reception. She works with great concentration in order to get the sharpest signal she can.

She returns to the mirror and investigates the spot she smeared cream on before. She feels it, runs her finger over it, and rubs some more cream on it.

Then she takes the rest of the water off the stove and pours it into the sink. She adds some more cold water. She goes to the closet, gets some nylon stockings, puts them into the sink and washes them.

She drapes a hand towel, taken from the towel rack next to the sink, over the back of the second chair, and very carefully hangs the stockings over it to dry.

As she is draining the water she washes out the sink and does a little dance step to the music. Then she leaves the room to close the window in the lavatory and comes back.


## Part Three

From the large closet she takes a do-it-yourself wall hanging that is almost finished. She lays it out over the back of the other chair and contemplates it. She pulls at something on it. Then she clears the whole table—she puts the ashtray on the sideboard and the cigarettes and lighter next to it. She drinks the last of the juice and puts the glass on the counter.

Then she spreads out the rug on the table. She pulls a heavy piece of iron out from under the sofa and sets it on top of the rug so that it won't slide around. She goes back to the closet and takes down a small wooden box, puts it on the table, goes to the sideboard, opens the drawer, and takes a pattern out. In the other drawer she keeps her scissors, which she gets out as well.

She arranges everything on the table and turns the floor lamp on. She tries out the light and decides to turn the large overhead light on, too. To switch it on, she crosses over to the light switch by the door.

She sits in the other chair, adjusts it to suit her, and begins to work after taking the wool and the needles out of the box.

Carefully she looks at the pattern, although she doesn't spread it out all the way, counts the knots, threads the needle, arranges the rest of the needles, and begins to work.

She works very painstakingly, with precision and expertise. Every time she finishes with one color, according to the pattern, she puts

*Farmyard & Other Plays*

down the needle, cuts the thread with the scissors, and trims the leftover piece of thread on the rug. *(In the staging one must work out exactly the making of do-it-yourself rugs.)*

After a while she gets up and puts on some more water, after which she returns to her work. When the water boils she goes to the sideboard, gets a tea bag and the teapot, and fixes herself some tea. She puts it on the counter, gets a cup, and sets it next to the pot. Then she works some more.

After a while, when the tea has steeped enough, she pours herself a cup, gets some sugar out of the sideboard, stirs it in, and takes the tea with her to the table. She gets a box of cookies out of the chest of drawers which she also puts on the table next to the rug.

She continues working, eating two or three cookies, drinking the cup of tea, and pouring herself a second cup after she finishes the first.


## Part Four

Gradually her interest in the work begins to wane noticeably. She blinks often; compares her work with the pattern for a disproportionately long time. She stops working, gets a cigarette, her lighter, and the ashtray from the sideboard, puts the things on the table, and smokes a cigarette without working.

She returns to her rug, but works restlessly and with distraction and irritation. She stands up, takes her wrist watch out of the bowl, and looks to see how late it is. She goes over to the radio and turns it down. Then she sits again and continues to work, more slowly this time but still efficiently. She gets up again, takes the empty tea cup and puts it on the counter. She runs water into the tea pot, rinses it out, and throws the used tea bag into the garbage can under the counter.

She gets the ashtray, empties it into the can, wipes it with a cloth, and puts it on the sideboard. Then she goes to the mirror and contemplates herself in it. She seems satisfied.

She returns to the table and sits. She studies the pattern carefully, counts, and then works very quickly and exactly until she finishes the rug, even though there is no real way of telling that it is finished. She puts the needles in the box, folds up the pattern, lays the scissors with it; then she stand up and surveys her work from a distance. *(To make a wall hanging 45 cm. by 70 cm.—approx. 18" × 28"—one must work an hour a day for about a month-and-a-half to two months.)* She smiles, takes the rug and spreads it out over the width of the couch by the wall, to take a look at it. She moves back as far away from it as possible and examines her work critically and for a long time. She is satisfied.

Lovingly she takes the rug and hangs it over the other chair without folding it up.

Then she begins to clean up the things on the table, putting them back in exactly the same order she took them out.

After she has finished this, she takes another contented but cautious look at her finished wall hanging and picks at it one more time. The only effect of her picking is that she looks at it anxiously to see if she hasn't ruined it.

## Part Five

Fred Rauch signs off; his program is over. Clearly one recognizes that Fräulein Rasch has heard this. She turns off the radio before another program is announced.

She goes to the window and carefully pulls the curtain back, staring out. At length she locks the window and pulls the shade down so that no one can look in.

Finally she sets the table for the next day. By the eggcup, etc., one can tell that she is preparing the table for breakfast.

Then she opens up her hide-away bed. *(It would be best to have a convertible couch with the bedlinen stored in a box underneath.)*

The ritual of body maintenance begins. This goes from hair curling to foot care, from deodorant spray to toothbrushing. Everything is done with tremendous thoroughness.

She observes a strict regimen with her underwear as well. Her panties are put with her dirty clothes in a laundry bag in the closet, and a fresh pair is laid out for the next morning. She also selects the clothes she will wear for the next day, which she hangs neatly on the outside wall of the closet. The personal things she lays on the empty seat of the chair. All the other clothes she puts in the closet so that they can hang out and be worn again.

She pulls a warm attractive nightgown out from between the sheets, draws it on, and puts a dressing gown on over it. Then she goes to the toilet. This time she only has to urinate; nevertheless she wipes herself neatly with toilet paper and opens the window a crack. She comes back into the room and washes her hands again.

Then she begins her security check. She double locks the door, makes sure the gas is turned off, the garbage can tightly closed, and the faucet not dripping. Carefully she opens the window, spending a long time to make sure that it is at the proper height and that air can come in so that she can pull the shade again.

Then she sets up her temporary night table. She pulls a cloth-covered stool out from behind the back of the couch.

On it is set an alarm clock, a book, an empty glass, and a magazine.

She takes the glass, rinses it out, fills it with fresh water, and puts it back in its place on the table.

She sits down on the edge of the bed, picks up the alarm clock, winds it up, and sets it for six o'clock. She tries it to make sure it works; and then, satisfied, she puts it back.

Not too long after, she gets up again, turns off the big light, looks around the room, takes off her robe, and lays it across the foot of the bed.

Then she lies down in bed. In doing so, she is very careful and does not lie comfortably because she has to watch out for her hair curlers.

She picks up the book, looks for her place, finds it, but she does not read; she just stares ahead of her. This lasts for quite some time. Then she lays the book down, looks around the room once more, and turns off the light.

At first she lies quietly; then she turns around carefully because of the hair curlers and tries to sleep.

Finally she makes an extremely restless movement in bed and turns the light on. She gets up, puts her robe back on, unlocks the door, and goes to the toilet—all of this very quietly. In the toilet she closes the window. She returns to the room, locks the door behind her, washes her hands, and dries them. Then she walks over to the rug and takes another look at it.

A few moments later she goes to the sideboard, opens the top drawer, and takes out a box of pills. She takes them to the table, puts them down, gets the glass of water from the night table, and sets it down next to the pills.

Cautiously she sits down on the chair with her stockings, without leaning back, so as not to wrinkle them. She takes a pill out and swallows it with a sip of water. From the box she removes the dosage sheet and reads it through.

She opens the box all the way and lets all the pills spill out. She counts them out in two rows. There are nine pills left from a box of twenty. Slowly she takes one after another, until the water which she swallows in small sips is all gone. She gets up to go to the sink, stops, goes to the refrigerator, takes out a small bottle of wine which is half full, returns to the table, opens the bottle, pours a little into the glass, and takes the rest of the pills. Then she waits a bit.

She pours the rest of the wine into the glass. It spills over and runs onto the tablecloth. She lifts up the glass and wipes the spot off with the sleeve of her robe. She sips the wine.

Then she waits quietly and thoughtfully, but presently one can detect a sign of interest in her face.

Pause, then

# Farmyard

## A Play In Three Acts

### English Version By
### Michael Roloff & Jack Gelber

First American Performance:

Yale Drama School, Winter, 1975

| | |
|---|---|
| *Director:* .................... | ......Jack Gelber |
| *The Farmer:* ................... | ...James Zitlow |
| *His Wife:* ..................... | ...Edith Tarbesco |
| *Beppi:* ....................... | .Marcel Rosenblatt |
| *Sepp:* ....................... | ....Wynston Jones |
| *Assistant Director:* ............. | ....Denise Gordon |
| *Technical Director:* ............. | ......Drew Kafka |
| *Lighting:* .................... | .......Brian Lago |
| *Dramaturg:* ................... | .....Dragon Klaic |

**Characters:**
the FARMER, his WIFE, BEPPI, SEPP, a DOG (female)
**Scenery:**
Extremely sparse, all of it movable. Simultaneous scenery for each act.
Work light. Light changes, blackouts, only at the end of each act.
**A note to the director:**
It is very important for the piece that a dog take part in it. This should
be handled in the following manner: In Act I Scene 6, SEPP is alone
onstage with the dog; at other moments it is merely desirable to have
the dog appear every so often, but it is not absolutely essential. Since
the dog's behavior cannot be calculated into the dialogue it is up to
the director to improvise as best he can.

**Concerning the pauses:**
The piece, which is set in a farm environment, becomes clear and comprehensible only if the indicated pauses are strictly adhered to.

— = roughly five seconds

*(pause)* within the dialogue = caesura of roughly ten seconds

*(pause)* = silence of at least twenty seconds

*(long pause)* = silence of at least thirty seconds

*Intermission after Act II*

*Farmyard & Other Plays*

# ACT ONE

## Scene 1

*(Combination living room and kitchen. The* WIFE *is cooking.* BEPPI *with a picture postcard. Kitchen utensils.)*

| | |
|---|---|
| WIFE: | From your Godmother. Read it. |
| BEPPI: | Aunt Hilda. |
| WIFE: | She wrote you cause she thinks of you. |
| BEPPI: | Where is she? |
| WIFE: | Don't ask, just read it. |
| BEPPI: | *(reads)* My dear Beppi! *(smiles)* Ssssoon me are going. . . |
| WIFE: | *(gives her a slap)* What is that? |
| BEPPI: | *(reads)* Soon w-we are going to visit you *(smiles)* when me. . . . |
| WIFE: | *(like before)* Again! Open your eyes!! |
| BEPPI: | . . . we. . . .*(hesitates)* |
| WIFE: | What letter is that??? *(writes it large in the air)* |
| BEPPI: | T-t-t-t-t |
| WIFE: | You see! |
| BEPPI: | Me—we has—have time. *(brief pause, then quickly)* Your Godmother, Aunt Hilda. |
| WIFE: | Right. Now you've got it. *(turns back to her work)* |
| BEPPI: | *(looks at the front of the postcard, extended look. Turns the card around and reads it again, faultlessly.)* Dear Beppi! Soon we are going to visit you when we have time. Your Godmother, Aunt Hilda! |
| WIFE: | You're to dry the dishes!!! |

## Scene 2

*(*BEPPI *and* SEPP *at work in the stable. They are cleaning out dung.* BEPPI *could also be milking.)*

SEPP: And then—they welcomed the captain and said *(pause)* he should pick one out for himself. *(pause)* And then he didn't want to—And then his Indian friend said, the one who understood the language of the Indians, *(pause)* if he don't pick one it's an insult to the chief, and then he went down along into their camp *(pause)* and afterwards—they showed all of them to him. He didn't like any *(pause)* cause they had such funny faces, and afterwards he finally saw one he really liked—But afterwards the Indian chief let him know all right *(pause)* that he's picked the one who's been expelled from the tribe and that no one can touch her cause he gets sick otherwise *(pause)* but then he said: it's her or no one, and simply went up to her and embraced her. *(pause)* Afterwards the Indians all ran apart and said he would die now because he had touched her. *(long pause)* But that was all bullshit, just a superstition, and then of course he didn't die, but married her afterwards *(pause)* and when the wedding night was over and the two of them were still alive the Indians saw that he was right. *(pause)* I mean they felt that he—the "white man"—had supernatural powers and that he destroyed the bad magic. *(pause)* Afterwards all of them came and wanted him to become their medicine man. But because he was really a doctor he became the first white man the Indians trusted and let themselves be cured by. And then the woman he married said to him *(pause)* that the tribe had made a plan as revenge for the attack by the whites *(pause)* and afterwards he talked with them, and then they made him their deputy, and afterwards he worked out a ceasefire. And that's the way it was.

*(pause)*

BEPPI: And then!!?

## Scene 3

(SEPP *is sitting on the toilet, taking a shit and masturbating.*)

*Farmyard & Other Plays*

# Scene 4

*(In the room. Evening.* SEPP *and* THE FARMER *at the table.* THE WIFE *is cooking.* BEPPI *is playing with pieces of firewood.)*

SEPP:     I just ain't got no luck in life, that's it. If someone got no luck there's nothing can be done.

        *(pause)*

FARMER:   Everyone makes his own luck, they say.

SEPP:     Not everyone.

FARMER:   Excuses.

WIFE:     That's the way it is if he says so.

SEPP:     Right. That's something I'd know about—In six years I'm gonna retire, then my worries is over. That'd be a whole lot better then. If I'm lucky I'm gonna do it earlier.

FARMER:   If I was you I'd go out and get myself a steady job.

WIFE:     But he says it ain't easy!

        *(pause)*

FARMER:   We're having an economic boom!

WIFE:     Still.

FARMER:   Anyone who wants to work can work. When the harvest is in, you can go down to that unemployment place till they got something for you. That's it.

SEPP:     To find something steady ain't easy for me, the man at the unemployment office said, cause I ain't young no more. And that's it.

FARMER:   Just like a gypsy.

SEPP:     I used to have a steady job in the old days.

        *(pause)*

        Or if I was in the city, that'd be a whole lot better. But I ain't in the city.

FARMER:   You bet.

SEPP:     One time I was on a farm ten times the size of yours. A real farm, that was a REAL farm.

FARMER: Musta been a real spread.

SEPP: Right.

*(pause)*

FARMER: And why'd you leave it?

SEPP: Cause I wanted to go to the city.

FARMER: The city.

SEPP: That's right.

FARMER: Then what the hell are ya doing here?

SEPP: My, now that's hard to say.

WIFE: *(to* BEPPI*)* Don't pull the wood apart; it's for stoking the fire.

*(pause)*

FARMER: She's outgrown her dolls.

WIFE: It's a shame.

SEPP: She just wants to play.

WIFE: Shouldn't play no more, should do something real.

FARMER: Retarded she is.

WIFE: Retarded you are, you hear what your pa is saying? Ain't makin' us happy.

FARMER: Others your age already go to high school.

WIFE: When I was your age I was up in the mountain pastures.

SEPP: That was in the old days, wasn't it?

WIFE: Alone up in the mountains. I had to work hard all day; at night I was afraid. Once I almost came down, but then I didn't dare after all.

FARMER: There, you hear it?

WIFE: Give me the wood, have to stoke up. *(takes the pieces from* BEPPI, *puts them in the stove)*

BEPPI: Don't burn Dollie.

WIFE: Set the table, we gonna eat now.

*(pause)*

SEPP: It's bad if someone can't see proper.

WIFE: Can see all right cause she got glasses.

FARMER: The fourth pair . . . cause they're free.

WIFE: Would have everything if she wasn't retarded.

SEPP: I can still see with no glasses. And read the papers.

| | |
|---|---|
| FARMER: | Ain't none of us ever got bad eyes, only her. |
| | *(they start to eat)* |
| BEPPI: | It's county fair time now. |
| WIFE: | Eat and shut up. |

# Scene 5

*(The stable in the evening.* SEPP *and* BEPPI *watch cats at play. They're working.)*

| | |
|---|---|
| SEPP: | All cats look the same at night. |
| | *(long pause)* |
| SEPP: | You see them, the two? |
| BEPPI: | *(nods)* |
| SEPP: | Which is the one and which is the other? |
| BEPPI: | *(looks)* |
| SEPP: | *(smiles)* |
| | *(pause)* |
| SEPP: | The left one is the one who's red and the right one's the other. |
| BEPPI: | *(nods)* |
| SEPP: | So you can see! |
| | *(pause)* |
| SEPP: | Everyone sees what the Lord gives him to see. |
| | *(pause)* |
| SEPP: | Now they're fighting, you see? |
| BEPPI: | *(nods)* |
| SEPP: | You can see everything? |
| | *(pause)* |
| BEPPI: | No more now. |
| SEPP: | Well, it's over now. Now they're starting. |
| | Now he's jumping her, you see? |
| | *(pause)* |

Farmyard

SEPP: Look. . . . It's her own fault she lets him, the tomcat's only a year old, right?

BEPPI: *(nods)*

*(pause)*

SEPP: What's young is desirable. I don't like them, the young ones. *(he laughs)*

*(pause)*

## Scene 6

*(Evening.* SEPP *in his room with his dog, which is eating. Watching the dog.)*

SEPP: Come on, eat. *(pause)* Don't you like it? *(pause)* I got nothing else. *(pause)* And if I did you wouldn't get it. Cause you can't pick and choose.

*(pause)*

If you don't eat it, I'll give it to the cat. Then you can see where you go if you get hungry. A good dog eats what's put in front of him, don't you know that?

*(pause)*

He's picky, that's what.

# ACT II

## Scene I

*(A small county fair, early afternoon, a dead time.* BEPPI *and* SEPP. BEPPI *completely fascinated.* SEPP *slightly drunk.)*

SEPP: You gotta wish?

BEPPI: *(doesn't react)*

SEPP: Want to ride the merry-go-round? *(It's a ghost train)* You afraid? Look at those big dolls.

BEPPI: *(afraid, fascinated)*

SEPP: Come, let's take a ride.

*(takes her by the hand to the box office)*

SEPP: One adult and one child.

*(they take the ghost train)*

*(return)*

BEPPI: *(disturbed)*

SEPP: It was nice wasn't it?

BEPPI: *(uncertain)*

SEPP: What's the matter?

BEPPI: *(walks stiffly)*

SEPP: Something hurting you?

BEPPI: *(denies it)*

SEPP: You dirtied your pants. You did. Come on now. Were you scared?

BEPPI: *(completely confused)*

SEPP: Or was it the soda pop? Come on we'll clean you up. *(They go behind a tent or away from the crowd.)* Here, wipe yourself with these leaves.

*(She cleans herself; diarrhea runs down her legs.)*

SEPP: You shit in your pants. Here let me. *(He cleans her up.)* Take off your pants, you can't run around like that. (BEPPI *cleans herself with his help.)* Wipe yourself with this. Here

let me. *(He takes his handkerchief and wipes her with it.)*
It's all right again. *(pause)* Come here.

*(He takes her and deflowers her.)*

# Scene 2

*(In* SEPP'S *room.* SEPP *and* BEPPI.*)*

SEPP: *(gives* BEPPI *a purse)* This is for you. From the city.

BEPPI: *(looks)*

SEPP: Say if you don't like it and I'll take it back.

BEPPI: No.

SEPP: Well, doesn't a person say "thank you" or not?

BEPPI: Thank you.

SEPP: So that you see that there is someone who thinks of you. *(looks at the purse himself)* That wasn't cheap, you can say that again. Genuine leather. *(puts a dollar inside)* There, so you have a start.

BEPPI: *(takes the purse)*

SEPP: When the time comes when you have money—so you don't lose it.

BEPPI: *(smiles)*

# Scene 3

*(A restaurant that extends into a garden outdoors.* SEPP *and* BEPPI *arrive on a motorscooter.* BEPPI *on the back seat. They get off and go into the garden, etc.)*

SEPP: *(while dismounting)* Did I go too fast?

BEPPI: *(denies that he did)*

SEPP: Want me to go slower on the way home?

BEPPI: No.

*(pause)*

BEPPI: I like to drive with you.

*(They go into the garden.)*

*(sit down at a table)*

SEPP:    We won't eat nothing, costs too much.

BEPPI:  *(nods in agreement)*

SEPP:    Or do you want a hot dog?

BEPPI:  *(denies that she does)*

*(pause)*

SEPP:    It's nice here, isn't it?

BEPPI:  *(nods)*

SEPP:    You like it?

BEPPI:  Yes.

*(pause)*

SEPP:    You can have a hot dog if you want.

BEPPI:  A soda.

SEPP:    Ain't you hungry?

BEPPI:  No . . . soda.

*(SEPP looks around; no one's coming.)*

SEPP:    I'm gonna have a beer. I'm gonna go inside cause no one's serving out here.
Coming?

BEPPI:  *(nods)*

SEPP:    *(goes inside the restaurant)*

BEPPI:  *(uncertain, looks around. Then straightens her dress, neckerchief, pulls up her knee socks, etc. Then folds her hands on the table.)*

SEPP:    *(comes back)*
It's coming right away. *(He sits back down.)*

*(long pause)*

In five years if I'm lucky—I'm gonna retire *(pause)* then I'm a free man. No one's gonna tell me what to do, no way, nothing, no way.

*(long pause)*

Then I'm going to the city and get an apartment. Afterward you can come if you like.

*(pause)*

To the apartment, in the city.

BEPPI:  The city.

SEPP:    Right, the city. At the outskirts cause it's cheaper there. You got the most luck and opportunities in the city. They want people there. Everywhere. They don't even check who it is; they're happy with anyone they got.

*(pause)*

SEPP: One day you'll understand what I'm telling you. Time passes faster than you think. You just turn around and a year is over.

BEPPI: *(turns and looks around)*

# Scene 4

*(In a shed.* SEPP *and* BEPPI *together after sexual intercourse.)*

SEPP: I didn't mean to hurt you. Couldn't be helped.

BEPPI: *(denies it)*

SEPP: Of course not.

BEPPI: Why?

SEPP: Cause that's the way it is; you don't understand that. *(pause)*

BEPPI: Do unto others as you want them to do unto you.

SEPP: *(remains silent)*

*(pause)*

SEPP: That's different.

*(pause)*

SEPP: What're you looking for?

BEPPI: Glasses.

SEPP: Won't find 'em no more.

BEPPI: *(nods)* They're where you put them.

BEPPI: Where?

SEPP: I see them.

BEPPI: *(looks)*

SEPP: Close.

BEPPI: Where?

SEPP: Gotta say "please."

BEPPI: Please.

SEPP: You're cold . . . cold . . . warm . . . warmer. . . .

| | |
|---|---|
| BEPPI: | *(smiles)* Play? |
| SEPP: | Cold.—Cold.—Warmer.—Cold.—Warmer.—Warm.—Very warm. So hot you're gonna burn yourself. |
| BEPPI: | Where? |
| SEPP: | Real hot. You don't look nice with glasses. |
| BEPPI: | Want to see? |
| SEPP: | No need to look now. |
| BEPPI: | . . . red. |
| SEPP: | That's normal. Doesn't matter. It'll stop again. You'll see. It's like I said. |
| BEPPI: | When? |
| SEPP: | When it's over. *(pause)* Tomorrow. |
| BEPPI: | *(nods)* |
| SEPP: | *(uncertain)* |
| | *(pause)* |
| SEPP: | Now I'm gonna go out, so no one notices that I'm gone. |
| BEPPI: | Stay. |
| SEPP: | You can stay a little if you want, I'll keep a lookout. Then you can come out too. |
| | *(gets up and goes out)* |
| BEPPI: | Glasses. *(looks for them)* |

## Scene 5

*(In the room. WIFE and BEPPI. BEPPI nicely dressed.)*

| | |
|---|---|
| WIFE: | Let me look at you. |
| BEPPI: | *(lets her)* |
| WIFE: | Yes. You're pretty. All you need now is a ribbon, then you can march off. |
| BEPPI: | *(nods)* |
| WIFE: | *(ties a ribbon around her braids)* |
| WIFE: | Now go on, and after confession come straight home. To help me make jam. |
| BEPPI: | Yes. |

| WIFE: | Now get going. |
|---|---|
| BEPPI: | Good-bye. |
| WIFE: | Don't be gone forever. |
| | (BEPPI *goes off.*) |
| | (WIFE *gets ready to make jam.*) |

## Scene 6

*(In the field, lying down.* BEPPI *and* SEPP.*)*

| BEPPI: | Had to confess. |
|---|---|
| SEPP: | Of course, but ya didn't say with who. |
| BEPPI: | "I was unchaste." |
| SEPP: | Right. That's enough—Is no one's business, just ours. And we ain't gonna let ourselves be asked questions of by nobody. |
| | (*pause*) |
| SEPP: | Now we do it. |
| BEPPI: | Later. |
| SEPP: | Don't want to? Make an effort. All you need is a little good will. |
| BEPPI: | Tell something. |
| SEPP: | Afterwards I'll tell you a story, if you're a good girl to me. |
| | (BEPPI *undresses herself.*) |
| | It's over in a jiffy now. It's over before you even notice. |
| | (*pause*) |
| BEPPI: | Was confessed already. |
| | (*pause*) |
| SEPP: | And what'd the priest say? |
| BEPPI: | Six Our Fathers and two Aves. |
| SEPP: | Confessed everything? |
| BEPPI: | (*nods*) Otherwise a mortal sin. |
| SEPP: | Right. How'd you say it? |
| BEPPI: | First Commandment: Thou shalt love and honor the Lord thy Father. Second Commandment: Thou shalt love and honor |

father and mother. I made trouble for father and mother. Third Commandment: Sundays and holidays. Fourth Commandment: I've never cursed, never. Fifth Commandment: . . . Sixth Commandment: I was unchaste.

SEPP: How'd you say it?

BEPPI: Sixth Commandment: I was unchaste.

SEPP: Nothing else?

BEPPI: That I lied.

SEPP: The priest ask something?

BEPPI: Nothing.

SEPP: Penance?

BEPPI: Six Our Fathers and two Aves.

SEPP: Did you do it?

BEPPI: Ten Our Fathers and three Aves.

SEPP: You're real eager!

BEPPI: (smiles)

SEPP: You did real well. (He pats her.)

BEPPI: (smiles)

SEPP: Now everything's forgiven and forgotten. You'll see.

BEPPI: (nods)

(starts coitus)

SEPP: You're a real good girl.

(BEPPI emits a few sounds; she has an orgasm.)

SEPP: Be quiet so that no one hears nothing—Don't you hear me?

BEPPI: (doesn't hear)

SEPP: (uncertain, stops) Did I hurt you? Didn't want to—be quiet, afterwards I'll tell you a story.

(pause)

BEPPI: A real nice one!

# Scene 7

(FARMER and SEPP in SEPP'S room.)

FARMER: That's gonna cost you ten years and me my honor.

SEPP:      But not cause it was on purpose.

FARMER:    That's a big help.

           *(long pause)*

FARMER:    It leaves you speechless.

           *(pause)*

FARMER:    And we put our trust in him.

SEPP:      That's the way it goes.

FARMER:    Three months.

SEPP:      No one counted the days.

           *(pause)*

FARMER:    Want to know a secret? She's pregnant.

SEPP:      Why?

FARMER:    She just is.

SEPP:      That ain't true, that's a lie.

FARMER:    We have proof.

SEPP:      Not possible.

FARMER:    You bet.

SEPP:      Nothing is.

FARMER:    We had to make a test. Cost ten dollars.

SEPP:      Why?

FARMER:    It's made with piss.

SEPP:      Whose?

FARMER:    Hers.

SEPP:      At the doctor's?

FARMER:    At the doctor's; what do you know? At the drugstore. They
           do it with a frog. They shoot piss into the frog and then he
           changes color. That's it.

SEPP:      I didn't know that.

FARMER:    Now you do. If she's pregnant it changes color.

SEPP:      Did it change color?

FARMER:    Right. That's proof of pregnancy.

           *(pause)*

SEPP:      But it wasn't on purpose.

FARMER:    Cause you're a pig, no two ways about that.

SEPP:     Yeah, right.

FARMER:   We'll also tell the priest. We'll tell everyone.

SEPP:     I'm leaving.

FARMER:   Where you going?

SEPP:     To the city.

          *(pause)*

FARMER:   We'd never have hired you if we'd known.

SEPP:     Leaving anyhow.

FARMER:   You'll stay a while yet. There's got to be a punishment. You'll see.

SEPP:     What?

FARMER:   Just you wait and see.

          *(pause)*

FARMER:   An underage child and retarded. It leaves you speechless.

SEPP:     Didn't want to, I swear.

FARMER:   Couldn't find nobody else? You don't shit where you eat, and a child besides. . . .

SEPP:     Didn't dare never nowhere.

FARMER:   Why?

SEPP:     Won't say.


# Scene 8

*(In the stable. Young cats in the corner.* SEPP *and* BEPPI.*)*


SEPP:     That's a nice litter. But only one can stay.

BEPPI:    *(looks at the animals)*

SEPP:     Just the way small cats are. Pick one out.—Since you gave me away, you'll see what that gets you.

BEPPI:    *(looks)*

SEPP:     Which one you want?

BEPPI:    Nothing.

SEPP:     They're all the same. But one of them gets caught.

BEPPI:    EENNIE, MEENIE, MINEE, MOE,

Catch a tiger by the toe
If he hollers, make him pay
fifty dollars every day. This one!

SEPP: Yours it is. Pa and Ma know everything now.

BEPPI: *(looks)*

SEPP: You gave me away.

BEPPI: Nothing. Mama knew.

SEPP: You tell her?

BEPPI: *(denies it)*

SEPP: Believe you, sure.


# Scene 9

*(In the yard.* SEPP *and* FARMER.*)*


FARMER: What are you looking at? No work to do?

SEPP: The dog.

FARMER: Your dog ain't on my yard.

SEPP: Where else she gonna be?

FARMER: It'll be somewhere all right.

SEPP: Can't a person look?

FARMER: You got nothing left to look at in my yard.

SEPP: Right.

FARMER: There, you knew it.

*(pause)*

SEPP: I'm just looking for my dog.

FARMER: Then look for her. "Seek and ye shall find."

SEPP: Right.

FARMER: Was here.

SEPP: Where?

FARMER: By the barn.

SEPP: Why?

FARMER: Ask her yourself. No concern a dog that don't belong to me.

SEPP: She's a roamer, that's it.

FARMER:   You'll find her all right.
          (*pause*)
FARMER:   And if I catch you on my farm once more I'll blow your head off; now you knows it.
SEPP:     You don't have no gun.
FARMER:   You'd be the one to know.
          (*pause*)
SEPP:     I'm just looking for my dog.
FARMER:   Yeah.
SEPP:     (*by the barn*) There she is. Nell! Nell! Come here. (*whistles*) Heel! Don't you hear me? You want a kick????
          (*The dog is dead.*)
FARMER:   Found her?
SEPP:     Yeah, that's her. . . .
FARMER:   Then make sure you get going, the two of you.
SEPP:     . . . Murderer.
FARMER:   Probably ate some rat poison; there was some laid out in the barn.
SEPP:     (*picks up the dead dog*)
          Let's go home. (*goes away with the dog*)
FARMER:   That does it.

# Scene 10

(*In* SEPP'S *room.* SEPP *is packing his stuff into a small bag.* BEPPI.)

SEPP:     No need to look inside, it's nothing for you.
BEPPI:    Want to.
SEPP:     She's in there.
BEPPI:    I know. (*looks inside the bag*)
SEPP:     (*stops the pacing*) You see her?
BEPPI:    (*nods*)
SEPP:     She's dead?

| | |
|---|---|
| BEPPI: | *(nods)* |
| SEPP: | Nothing can be done anymore, eh? |
| BEPPI: | *(agrees)* Nothing no more. |
| SEPP: | *(cries)* Just go, don't need you no more. |
| BEPPI: | *(smiles)* Pretty dog. *(affirms it)* |
| SEPP: | Everything's done. Go on now. |
| BEPPI: | *(shakes her head, yes and no, stands up, walks around the table, looks uncertain; then she takes the things and helps pack)* |
| SEPP: | What ya doing? |
| BEPPI: | nothing *(stops again)* |
| | *(pause)* |
| SEPP: | Everything's over but the shouting. |
| BEPPI: | Why? |
| SEPP: | It's over. |
| BEPPI: | I'm with you. |
| SEPP: | A lot of good that does me. |
| BEPPI: | *(nods)* |
| SEPP: | You got no right; you're nothing; that's it. |
| BEPPI: | *(nods)* |
| SEPP: | Now I'm going to the city to report what happened. |
| BEPPI: | Stay. |
| SEPP: | You don't need me; you'll be all right by yourself. |
| BEPPI: | Please. |
| SEPP: | Nothing keeps me here now the dog is dead. |
| BEPPI: | I'm askin' real nice. |
| SEPP: | No way. |
| | *(pause)* |
| SEPP: | *(starts to pack again)* |
| BEPPI: | Comin' back? |
| SEPP: | When you get the child I'll come look if it's turned out good. |
| BEPPI: | Don't go, stay. |
| SEPP: | It's over between us. |
| BEPPI: | Why? |
| | *(pause)* |

SEPP:      Bought a chocolate for you.

BEPPI:     *(takes it, cries)*

SEPP:      No need to cry.

BEPPI:     No need.

# ACT III

## Scene I

*(On the way to church in bad weather.* FARMER *and* WIFE. BEPPI *slightly in front.)*

FARMER: Can people see something already?

> *(pause)*

WIFE: Can't see nothin' yet.

> *(long pause)*

FARMER: I see something.

WIFE: That's your imagination. There's nothing to see.

FARMER: No one should ever see nothing.

WIFE: Don't worry.

> *(long pause)*

WIFE: They say someone who's slightly off doesn't feel death the way we do.

FARMER: Of course a fly don't feel nothing either.

> *(pause)*

WIFE: Fifth Commandment: thou shalt not kill.

FARMER: Sixth: thou shan't be unchaste.

> *(pause)*
>
> That's something between me and the Lord.
>
> *(pause)*

WIFE: They say the child goes on living in the mother's belly for hours after.

FARMER: Not this one.

> *(long pause)*

WIFE: I wouldn't forget that my whole life. I know that.

FARMER: God helps those who help themselves.

WIFE: Yes.

> *(pause)*

WIFE: Blessed are the meek, for theirs is the kingdom of heaven.

FARMER: I don't believe that.

*Farmyard & Other Plays*

| | |
|---|---|
| WIFE: | The ideas people get. It's unheard of. |
| FARMER: | Just talking. |
| WIFE: | But to go into your ruin with your eyes wide open, that's not right either. |
| FARMER: | No. |
| WIFE: | When one thinks about it. |
| FARMER: | I know that my daughter who's still a child that's retarded shouldn't be pregnant by an old bum. What would people say? No! |
| WIFE: | Why a bum? |
| FARMER: | That's what you say. |

## Scene 2

*(Daytime, in the kitchen. The centrifuge is attached to the bench.* BEPPI *is churning. The* WIFE *is wet-mopping the floor.)*

| | |
|---|---|
| WIFE: | That's no way to make butter, just mush. |
| BEPPI: | *(churns)* |
| | *(long pause)* |
| WIFE: | Pick it up. |
| BEPPI: | It's heavy. |
| WIFE: | Didn't used to be heavy for you.—You'll have to lick up what you spill. |

## Scene 3

*(Evening in the room.* FARMER *at the table with his paper.* WIFE. BEPPI *writes in a notebook.)*

| | |
|---|---|
| FARMER: | Whatcha doing? *(to* WIFE*)* |
| | *(pause)* |
| | *(to* BEPPI*)* What's the matter? *(to* WIFE*)* She belongs in bed. |
| WIFE: | Leave her be, she's doing her homework. |
| FARMER: | At night! |

| | |
|---|---|
| BEPPI: | Handwriting. |
| WIFE: | She's been good. |
| | *(pause)* |
| FARMER: | *(to* WIFE*)* Whatcha doing? |
| WIFE: | I'm makin' a solution. |
| FARMER: | What for? |
| | *(pause)* |
| WIFE: | You'll see. |
| | *(pause)* |
| FARMER: | Wanna do it? |
| WIFE: | Talk he can, that's all. |
| | *(pause)* |
| FARMER: | And if she doesn't do it? |
| WIFE: | She's gotta obey. |
| FARMER: | That doesn't help any. |
| WIFE: | Know something better? |
| BEPPI: | *(listens)* |
| WIFE: | Do your homework and don't bother about what don't concern you. |
| | *(pause)* |
| FARMER: | Everybody would do it if they knew it would work. |
| WIFE: | Cause it ain't usual, most folks don't know about it. |
| | *(pause)* |
| | *(*FARMER *goes on reading the paper.)* |
| WIFE: | Well *(to the* FARMER*)* go outside now; we do that amongst ourselves. We don't need no Peeping Toms. |
| FARMER: | *(gets up)* Going anyhow since that's your business. |
| | *(goes offstage)* |
| WIFE: | Well, we'll get it over with in no time at all. |
| BEPPI: | *(looks)* |
| WIFE: | Come here now. Take down your pants, lie down there. |
| BEPPI: | Noo. |
| WIFE: | We gotta wash so the dirt goes off; take down your pants. |
| BEPPI: | *(does it)* |

*Farmyard & Other Plays*

WIFE: Cause you have made such a mess that the dirt has to go out where it came in—That pinches a little but that don't matter, that's the soap that cleans everything. Pull up your skirt and spread your legs.

BEPPI: *(has undressed completely, stands there)*

WIFE: You're freezing, you dumbhead.

*(pause)*

WIFE: *(takes the rag from the stove, the scrub brush, wets it in the soap solution and proceeds to scrub the floorboards)*

*(pause)*

WIFE: Well, can't you hear what I said? You're supposed to go wash yourself outside in the tub, and then straight to bed, you gotta be up again by tomorrow.—I got my work to do.

# Scene 4

*(Night.* WIFE *and* FARMER *in their double bed.)*

WIFE: I tried my best, that's for sure. I can't blame myself anymore, that's for sure.

FARMER: Did I say something?

*(long pause)*

WIFE: That's the way it is; there's nothing one can do.

FARMER: No we can't. Other people can; others know how to help themselves.

WIFE: If it's no use, then it's no use.

FARMER: That's what I thought right away, that it makes no sense.

WIFE: Right.

*(pause)*

FARMER: If we had another child, a boy, at least that would be a real comfort.

WIFE: Why?

FARMER: It's obvious, ain't it?

WIFE:     When I couldn't get a second child when I was young I'm sure not gonna get one now; everybody knows that.
          *(pause)*
FARMER:   I can think out loud if I want to, can't I?
WIFE:     Yup.

## Scene 5

*(Hillside with cranberry bushes.* WIFE *and* BEPPI *are picking berries.* BEPPI *very pregnant.)*
          *(long pause)*
BEPPI:    *(has found a very productive spot)* So many!
WIFE:     *(smiles, softly)* Then pick 'em, and don't talk.
          *(pause)*

## Scene 6

*(Evening in the room.* WIFE *and* FARMER *and* BEPPI *having supper.)*
          *(long pause)*
BEPPI:    *(stops eating, looks at* FARMER *and* WIFE. *Her labor pains begin.)*
          *(pause)*
BEPPI:    Daddymommy.


CURTAIN

# Michi's Blood

## A Requiem

*English Version By*
*Michael Roloff & Denise Gordon*

First American Performance: Yale Drama School, Spring 1975.

*Director:* . . . . . . . . . . . . . . . . . . . . . . . . . . . . . . . . . . . .Denise Gordon
*Mary:* . . . . . . . . . . . . . . . . . . . . . . . . . . . . . . . .Marcel Rosenblatt
*Karl:* . . . . . . . . . . . . . . . . . . . . . . . . . . . . . . . . . . . . . .Andrew Davis

# I  TABLE CONVERSATION

MARY: Since we've only got this room you can go to the john.

KARL: It's cold in there.

MARY: Ya can't just take everything lyin' down.

KARL: Yeah.

MARY: Cause you're a filthy pig.

KARL: That's what you are; what's that make me?

MARY: You're crazy.

KARL: That's what you are;  what's that make me?

MARY: You're horny, but you can't get it together.

KARL: That's what you are; what's that make me?—I don't give a shit.

MARY: Don't eat if it don't taste. Think I'd stop ya?

KARL: Not you, cause I wouldn't ask.

MARY: Don't bother eatin' if it don't taste.

KARL: Tastes okay.

MARY: Ya don't love me no more. That's it.

KARL: If ya know it anyway.

MARY: That doesn't help none.

KARL: How's a body gonna eat in peace?

MARY: Am I botherin' you?

KARL: Not you for sure, cause I don't give a shit about ya!

MARY: It used to be different.

KARL: That's all over.

MARY: When ya need someone and he notices, then he don't know how ta appreciate that.—Want me ta leave ya alone?

KARL: I want my peace and quiet.

MARY: No one's sayin' nothin'.

KARL: I've had it.

MARY: Leave it, then we got somethin' for dinner.

KARL: A bitch if there ever was one. It makes me puke when I see it.

MARY: Go ahead, think I'd stop ya? No one asks me whether I like it or not.

KARL: Just you call me a shithead.

Michi's Blood

MARY: Shithead. Pig, you're a filthy pig. I'm gonna sic the cops on ya. They'll put ya where ya belong. And I worked my heart out for someone like that. That guy got no gratitude at all.

KARL: I'd do it again right now.

MARY: Why doncha?

KARL: Yeah.—Stop bawling if ya don't git what I say.

MARY: I understand ya all right.

KARL: Cause ya are dumb.

MARY: Better dumb than a pig.

KARL: I jist don't like it no more.

MARY: No one's asked whether they like it or not.

KARL: I've had enough.

MARY: No one's like ya. You're crazy; plain as day.

KARL: Ya can't do nothin' for it.

MARY: Yeah.

KARL: Shut up and keep out of things.

MARY: I've got my rights, too.

KARL: Ya got nothin'.

MARY: You're a drunk and a lush.

KARL: Yeah.

MARY: Antisocial ya are.

KARL: An old bag ya are.

MARY: A bum.

KARL: A slut.

MARY: I'm not.

KARL: Sure ya are.

## II REFLECTIONS ON LOVE

MARY: It's all over if ya gotta drag everythin' through the dirt.

KARL: Nothin's over.

MARY: You're taking advantage cause ya have me. Ya take it out on me cause ya don't like me no more, cause ya can't find another.

KARL: Cause I'm fed up with ya.

MARY: Don't think I don't know it. Don't think I'm stupid.

KARL: Ya'd talk different if ya knew the way ya looked.

MARY: Ain't got no mirror.

KARL: Go buy yaself one.

MARY: Ain't got no money.

KARL: Then I'll buy ya one.

MARY: It takes a while ta get ta know ya.

KARL: Now ya know it.

MARY: Then explain, cause no one can make ya out. What a prick he is.

KARL: Not cause I can help it.

MARY: Yeah, a person's still gotta know the score.

KARL: It stinks.

MARY: If only I hadn't got mixed up with ya.

KARL: Yeah, what if?

MARY: Won't say.

KARL: Cause ya can't think a nothin'.

MARY: Me, think a nothin'?

KARL: Yeah. Open your trap. Go on.

MARY: I'd have a lot ta say. Your ears'd perk up all right.

KARL: What's over is over.

MARY: There's nothin' left ta say. Right.—If a person knew the score, they'd know how ta change it. Ya better believe it.

KARL: That's a lot of help.

MARY: No need ta pick a fight now.

KARL: I never fight.

MARY: So you're coming?

KARL: Gonna let me?

MARY: Why not? All ya gotta have is a little good will. Nothin's so bad then.

KARL: Shut up.

MARY: Have already.


Michi's Blood

# III SOMETHING NEW

MARY: Your eyes are gonna pop when ya hear this.

KARL: That's what you think.

MARY: That's really somethin', cause I'm gettin a kid.

KARL: You're gettin' nothin'.

MARY: I ain't not got nothin', cause I'm pregnant with a kid.

KARL: Where?

MARY: There.

KARL: You a cat?

MARY: How do I know?

KARL: Why open your trap if ya don't know?

MARY: Why ain't I supposed ta open my trap? Somethin' 's coming. I went ta get myself tested; somethin' 's coming. It cost ten bucks. I'm just sayin'.

KARL: Ya think I'm nuts?

MARY: Don't ya wanna be a father?

KARL: Sure.

MARY: Then that's the way it is.

KARL: When?

MARY: It's been two months.

KARL: There's room for some happiness.

MARY: Yeah. A person doesn't always have ta think the worst.

KARL: Of course not.

MARY: You're gonna be a father.

KARL: Yeah.

MARY: Then it wasn't nothin'.

KARL: No. Ya gotta let people have a little happiness.

MARY: Yeah. Want nothin' but a little happiness.

# IV MAKING PLANS

MARY: Now that you're gonna be a father ya gotta change your ways.

KARL: Don't make my head spin.

MARY: Things ain't so bad once ya see a goal.

KARL: Cause ya see somethin'.

MARY: I see enough.

KARL: Things look good ta you.

MARY: Yeah.

KARL: Bawling, that's what ya can do.

MARY: I'm not sayin' nothin'.

KARL: Better not.

MARY: I believe you; you're the man, I'm the woman.

KARL: Yeah. Just ya don't forget it.

MARY: I'd like ta live on the sunny side; everythin' would be different then. But ya gotta put up with things as they are.

KARL: Right. Ya gotta fit in.

MARY: Yeah.

KARL: All cat's are gray at night; that's the truth, too.

MARY: Yeah.

## V ORDER IS RESTORED

MARY: You feel somethin'?

KARL: Yeah.

MARY: What?

KARL: A kid.

MARY: Sure. I feel it, too.

KARL: That's the feet, that's the belly, that's the head. Good enough?

MARY: Are ya kidding? I feel it when it kicks.

KARL: So do I.

MARY: That hurts, but it's nice.

KARL: Pain is pain.

MARY: Yes.

KARL: Then get rid of it.

MARY: You crazy or somethin'? I'd never, cause it's my happiness. Ya understand?

KARL: Ya should leave people their happiness.

MARY: That's right.

KARL: Open up now. It'll hurt, but that don't matter.

MARY: I can take it.

KARL: Cause ya got guts.

MARY: That's what I think. Now put it in. Ouch.

KARL: Told ya it stings.

MARY: Ouch.

KARL: Don't talk. Press together.

MARY: How long?

KARL: Until ya can't no more.

MARY: That'll take a while.

KARL: So much the better.

MARY: But it don't feel so good.

KARL: Who asks about that?

MARY: I know.

KARL: Feel somethin'?

MARY: Nothin' no more.

KARL: Then the effect's worn off. Let go.

MARY: Yeah. That's the difference. An animal can't put up a fight when it don't like somethin'.

KARL: We put up a fight.

MARY: Yeah.

KARL: Keep it open; now we're gonna do it again. If that doesn't help I don't know myself no more.

MARY: Doing is better than just thinking about it.

KARL: Yeah. Feel somethin'?

MARY: No pain no more.

KARL: Cause you're used ta it.

MARY: Ya get used ta everythin' they say.

KARL: Now ya can let go. All good things come in threes. A horse couldn't take that.

MARY: That's what I think. Inject it now. I'll hold still.

KARL: Feel nothin' at all?

MARY: It tickles.

KARL: It's all over with if ya can feel it.

MARY: That's what I think too. That's what it means.

*Farmyard & Other Plays*

KARL: Keep it shut, you're leaking.

MARY: Yeah, so that nothin' spills.—Why ain't ya sayin' nothin' no more?

KARL: Cause I'm waitin' for the effect.

MARY: Me too.

KARL: But soap is safe.

MARY: Tell me when it's enough.

KARL: Yeah. Let it out and everythin' is over and forgotten.

## VI SETTLING AND BALANCING THE SCORE

MARY: We all gotta go sometime.

KARL: Yeah. You're best off if ya ain't born, and second best if ya die young. So says Jesus.

MARY: I wouldn't sign my name ta that.

KARL: But that's what it says in the book.

MARY: Yeah.

## VII FUTURE AND COMMON SENSE

MARY: When d'ya think I'll be up again?

KARL: I got no crystal ball.

MARY: But it can't take long now.

KARL: Right. Since ya been lying down for a week.

MARY: It can't take no longer than that.

KARL: Takin' too long, is it?

MARY: It's stupid. Did ya see somethin'?

KARL: Nothin'.

MARY: But it's not there no more. I can feel that.

KARL: There was nothin' ta see. Take a look yourself if ya don't believe me.

MARY: I believe ya. One should never lose hope. Perhaps it just broke up.

KARL: How?

MARY: Everythin' breaks up in a soap solution.

KARL: Only in brine.

MARY: Also in brine.

KARL: But ya should be able ta see somethin'.

MARY: Then we'll just wait 'til the time comes.

KARL: Waitin' is stupid.

MARY: If ya see somethin', tell me. I'd like ta see what it looks like, at least once.

KARL: Ya need glasses for that.

MARY: Or a magnifying glass.

KARL: Yeah.

MARY: I'd be curious all right.

KARL: You're nuts.

## VIII WAITING

KARL: Whatcha lookin' at?

MARY: I ain't lookin', I'm thinkin'.

KARL: Nothin' important, that's for sure.

MARY: You'd be the one who'd know. Ya scared?

KARL: Ya gonna make a stink?

MARY: Not me.

KARL: Not me neither.

MARY: That's what ya think.

KARL: Cause I don't give a shit. But you're gonna kick off if ya don't stop bleedin' pretty soon.

MARY: You'd be the one ta know.

KARL: I know that for sure.—One can never be serious with ya. Ya know about nothin'.

MARY: You're just nervous. We'll make it.

KARL: That's for sure.

MARY: And no one knows nothing about no one.

KARL: Nothin'.

MARY: Yeah.

KARL: Ya can't look inside a person's brain.

MARY: No. Ya gotta have a crystal ball for that.

# IX ARRIVAL

KARL: You're supposed ta press.

MARY: I'm pressing.

KARL: The head or somethin' is showin' already. Hold on and press. Harder. It's coming. There it is.

MARY: Ya got it?

KARL: There it is.

MARY: Ya got it.

KARL: Take a look.

MARY: Ugly.

KARL: A corpse just ain't no child.—Whatcha got?

MARY: Somethin' else.

KARL: Is it never gonna stop?—A blob.

# X IT HAS BECOME QUIET

KARL: There's a reason for everythin'.

MARY: Yeah. If ya just know it.

KARL: Yeah.

# XI INFORMATION AND SECURITY

MARY: We gotta trust ourselves. Who else we got?

KARL: Right.

MARY: Yeah.

KARL: All you ever say is yeah.

MARY: What else should I say?

KARL: You'll think a somethin'.

MARY: If I keep thinkin'.

KARL: It's better if ya keep quiet, uses too much strength when ya talk.

MARY: I can take it all right.

KARL: Yeah. It'll be okay again. People die every day. That's the way it is.

MARY: That's the way it is. And if it was a girl, what'd we have called her?

KARL: Wouldn't have been no girl.

MARY: Cause I saw it.

KARL: Ya saw nothin'. Cause there was nothin' ta see.

MARY: I did too.

KARL: You're living in pictures.

MARY: Yeah?

KARL: You're just bein' ornery. Ya couldn't care less.

MARY: That's not true.

KARL: I got eyes.

MARY: Stupid is what ya are.

KARL: Yeah.

## XII THE EXPLANATIONS

KARL: A death that's got no meanin' is no murder. No one can tell me that.

MARY: I'm not sayin' nothin' and I won't let nobody tell me nothing either. Because I love ya.

KARL: No need to.

MARY: I should know. We gotta fit in.

KARL: That's what ya say.

MARY: I'm not sayin nothin'.—Ya just don't know me. It's really quiet now.

KARL: Afterwards we'll talk.

MARY: If ya could just think a something ta say. All ya gotta have is good will.

KARL: How?

MARY: Just like I said.

KARL: Ya wanna run that by me again?

## XIII FINDING THE TRUTH

MARY: Can I tell ya somethin'?

KARL: Why not?

MARY: I've got a pain.

*Farmyard & Other Plays*

KARL: Then pull yourself together. You'll manage; just don't think about it.

MARY: Yeah. One should never lose hope.

KARL: So what d'ya want?

MARY: I just don't know no more.

KARL: Probably somethin' stupid anyhow.

MARY: Yeah. Cause I forgot.

KARL: Always gotta add your two bits.

MARY: Why?

KARL: There.

MARY: I'm human too.

KARL: Christ. That's somethin'.

MARY: I'm tryin' to be serious.

KARL: Ya think I'm not? Ya think I'm any different?

MARY: I know that about you.

## XIV RESCUE ATTEMPTS

MARY: They say every minute some kid dies of hunger.

KARL: Want somethin'?

MARY: No. But a person's allowed to talk, right?

KARL: Talk is cheap, or doncha know that?

MARY: I don't wanna know.

KARL: Shut up.

MARY: It's easy tellin' someone like me, a person that's dyin', ta shut up.

KARL: Cause supposedly there's somethin' wrong with ya. What a joke.

MARY: You'd know.

KARL: Pickin' on me, that's all ya can do.

MARY: Can't even make a joke no more.

KARL: Ya don't do nothin' ta me, and I won't do nothin' ta you.

MARY: I didn't do nothin' ta you.

KARL: Ya would know.

MARY: If ya'd be straight with yourself you'd say ya did somethin' wrong.

KARL: Nothin'.

MARY: That proves nothin'.

KARL: Gonna take me ta court?

MARY: That's not what I meant.

KARL: If ya'd know anything, ya'd know there ain't nothin' ya can do wrong.—All ya gotta do is say if ya wanna fight.

MARY: Don't want to.

KARL: I know ya.

MARY: Not really.

KARL: And how.

MARY: I'd be curious all right.

## XV NO GOOD-BYES

MARY: Now come here once more.

KARL: What d'ya want? You're a real find.

MARY: And ya don't know what to do with me.

KARL: Right. Ya got guts.

MARY: Perhaps ya didn't need to do nothin' cause it would have come to nothing anyway.

KARL: Nobody knows nothing for certain.

MARY: Right. That's why.

KARL: Don't ya feel like talkin' no more?

MARY: I do.

KARL: Why bother if it's no good between us no more?

MARY: But we like each other, couldn't we?

KARL: Ya got a soft spot for me.

MARY: Ya ask stupid and ya get a stupid answer.

KARL: What now? Don't ya hear me? If ya can't hear ya gotta feel, understand?

**CURTAIN**

*Farmyard & Other Plays*

# Men's Business

(New version, 1973)

A PLAY IN EIGHT SCENES

For Ruth and Hans

*English Version by*
*Michael Roloff & Carl Weber*

Note about the new version: The play is not to be performed. This text has been rewritten to make it more accessible to the reader. F.X.K.

## Characters:

MARTHA, a professional butcher. She is between thirty and forty years of age, dark-haired, quite unattractive, and wears a butcher's coat most of the time.

OTTO, a worker (steel construction), roughly forty years old. Average type.

ROLFI, a German shepherd mongrel.

## The set:

A tripe shop which consists of the store, a small adjacent room, with the refrigeration room towards the back, where a small garden is assumed to be; the entrance is to the side.

The set should be constructed as a simultaneous set so scene changes won't be necessary.

# Scene 1

*(The table is festively set in the small room.* MARTHA *has dressed herself up a little.* OTTO *is coming directly from work. The shop is already closed.)*

OTTO: This sure is a ceremony.

MARTHA: You are supposed to enjoy it when you are with me. So, I don't hold anything back. That's caviar—costs $1.30 each little jar.

OTTO: Caviar; tastes like fish.

MARTHA: Fish eggs is what it is.

OTTO: Tiny eggs.

MARTHA: He lays millions of eggs like that, the fish does. Got to put butter on it. That really brings out the taste.

OTTO: Like royalty.

MARTHA: That's nothing. You can't really do things up in the shop. When you come to my place, your eyes will pop at what I can put out.

OTTO: It's nice here, too, if you aren't demanding.

MARTHA: Eat.

OTTO: You're spoiling me.

MARTHA: Eating is good for you. *(pause) (They eat.)*
I'd go to the movies if you weren't here.

OTTO: What's playing?

MARTHA: A sex-education film.

OTTO: Don't need that, know enough.

MARTHA: But a person can't know everything.

OTTO: To know everything spoils the fun.

MARTHA: You're the real thing, I knew that at once. *(pause)*

OTTO: Film people don't know anything about life either.

MARTHA: Right—I'm starting something new, a diary. Here, you can read what I wrote.

OTTO: So what are you writing?

MARTHA: Go ahead, read it.

OTTO: Fiction.

MARTHA: No. Not when I'm serious. I wrote about you.

OTTO: What'd you write about me?

MARTHA: That you have entered my life is what I wrote. Go ahead, read it. It's true.

OTTO: *(reads)* Right.

MARTHA: There, you see what I'm like. You can read everything I've written. I've no secrets from you. *(laughs)*

OTTO: I catch on to everything. *(pause)*

MARTHA: Had enough?

OTTO: Breakfast like a king, lunch like a businessman, supper like a bum—and you reach a ripe old age.

MARTHA: Then I'll clear the table.

*(While* MARTHA *clears the table* OTTO *lies down on the couch and takes a magazine from his briefcase.)*

MARTHA: *(after she's finished)* Whatcha got there?

OTTO: Nothing; men's business.

MARTHA: Nothing but naked chicks.

OTTO: It's not for you; men's business.

MARTHA: *(lies down beside him)* I want to see what's going on in the world. *(They look at the photos.)*

I like that one best.

OTTO: Average. There are better ones.

MARTHA: Are they hookers, to let their pictures be taken like that?

OTTO: You've got no idea what they are. Photo models; they ain't got nothing to do with hookers. Most of them go to college, and 'cause they can't pay for college they let their pictures be taken. Then they got money again and can live for another year.

MARTHA: So that's what they are like.

OTTO: Precisely, 'cause I know that.

MARTHA: And what do they earn when they get their pictures taken like that?

OTTO: Five thousand or more.

MARTHA: I would do that too and give up the shop.

*Farmyard & Other Plays*

OTTO:     No one would take your picture. Take a look at how they're stacked.

MARTHA:   That one ain't pretty either.

OTTO:     Still, there's a difference.

MARTHA:   If I'd be made up like that, and with a wig, you wouldn't recognize me.

OTTO:     I'd recognize you no matter what, I bet.

MARTHA:   That ain't necessary, 'cause I'm not broke the way they are.

OTTO:     You don't know about nothin'.

MARTHA:   But I've got an imagination.

OTTO:     Sure, that's something. *(They continue to leaf through the magazine.)*

MARTHA:   Got another magazine like that?

OTTO:     No; costs a buck.

MARTHA:   That's expensive.

OTTO:     I can splurge once a week. *(puts the magazine back into his briefcase)* Now you can take your things off; that's better.

MARTHA:   If that's what you want. *(OTTO watches her as she undresses. This takes quite a while.)*

          Aren't you going to take your things off?

OTTO:     We'll see. *(scratching and howling can be heard from the back door)*

MARTHA:   The dog wants to come in now.

OTTO:     Just what I expected, that he'd be acting up now. *(He gets up.)* Where's the leash?

MARTHA:   On top of the cupboard.

OTTO:     Filthy pig. *(He takes the leash from the closet, goes outside, beats the dog. Noises, etc.)*

MARTHA:   That dog is part of me, but you can beat it if you want to.

OTTO:     *(outside)* You filthy pig, shut up now.

MARTHA:   He gets impatient 'cause he's not used to being outside such a long time.

OTTO:     Scram, you pig.

MARTHA:   He's fond of me, he is.

OTTO:     *(returns) (The dog is silent.)* A pig is what that dog is. Sneaks between your legs, I've seen it.

MARTHA: He's jealous. That's normal.

OTTO: Yeah, a dog like no other.

MARTHA: I'm cold.

OTTO: Come here.

MARTHA: *(does so)*

OTTO: You fuss around like a virgin, and at your age.

MARTHA: I'm just not used to it the way you are.

OTTO: That's nature. *(on top of her)* You ain't pretty, but you're horny. *(pause)*

*(They make love.)*

## Scene II

*(MARTHA is wearing a white, slightly soiled butcher's coat. OTTO is smoking.)*

MARTHA: With a tripe shop you're always in business.

OTTO: Meat wherever you look.

MARTHA: You've got no idea what kinds of meat there are.

OTTO: Who cares.

MARTHA: If you knew about it, you could work for me. Need some help anyway.

OTTO: Do you think I'd stand around here all day long selling dog food?

MARTHA: I'd buy you a van and let you do the buying. A few hours in the morning at the slaughter house and you could spend the rest of the day in the sun. When you go to the market yourself, you've got better choice than when they just deliver, the way they do to me. But you've got to know your business. 'Cause buying is what can ruin you, or not.

OTTO: What do you pay?

MARTHA: We'd share everything.

OTTO: I'm earning more now.

MARTHA: How much?

OTTO: Eight hundred at least.

MARTHA: And what do they deduct?

OTTO: I'm talking about the net. You can never figure out what the gross is.

MARTHA: Then you've got more than I have.

OTTO: Steel construction workers are in demand. The firms lick their fingers if they've got a good gang working for them.

MARTHA: But I'm independent; that's something, too.

OTTO: What's the use of being independent if I can make more somewhere else?

MARTHA: But in winter all you do is collect unemployment.

OTTO: Winters I make sixty percent working the unemployment line of what I make in summer. And I don't move a finger.

MARTHA: My season is the winter season. Nothing spoils then, and when it gets cold people really start buying innards. Then I'm better off than you are.

OTTO: Would never have thought that you could live just from dog food.

MARTHA: Everything that eats meat. My father even catered to a circus.

OTTO: For the tigers. That's impressive.

MARTHA: But now where there are no more little circuses, there is nothing doing. Big ones wouldn't bother with me; they think in bigger quantities.

OTTO: You haven't even got any meat for people.

MARTHA: I could carry that too, particularly the innards, but then the Department of Health would get tough and I couldn't buy uninspected meat. But that would ruin the business. There are people who would buy the stuff and eat it. I know that but I don't ask no questions. Anyway, everything is in order here and I am really clean.

*(pause)*

OTTO: A lot of talking you can do. *(pause)* A woman as a butcher is abnormal anyway.

MARTHA: 'Cause I was physically retarded as a child and my parents had the butcher shop I just grew into it.

OTTO: Retarded, how?

MARTHA: Just an illness, it's over.

OTTO: Infectious?

MARTHA: Certainly not.

OTTO: Well, then it's all right.

MARTHA: I outgrew it long ago. That's what my parents said right away, that I'd outgrow it. Then she can take over the business and is in fine shape, that's what my parents said, where she's got nothing else to look forward to.

OTTO: The first time I came here I thought I'd shop here; it's cheap.

MARTHA: A lot of people think that.

OTTO: But they don't stick around the way I do.

MARTHA: Believe me, I've had my chances. With everybody who comes in here, day-in, day-out, but I've got my price, too.

OTTO: And where did you drop your virginity? If I may ask?

MARTHA: That's so long ago that I can't even remember.

OTTO: Just as well at your age.

MARTHA: Right. *(a pause)* When you're in the shop from morning til night, that takes it out of you. That doesn't leave you with much of a social life.

OTTO: Precisely. Nothing but dead critters all around you, no way to get any bright ideas.

MARTHA: Nobody knocks my business. That's my pride. A woman on her own doesn't have it easy. Everyone says so.

OTTO: You've got your dog.

MARTHA: We've always had a dog. As long as I can remember.

OTTO: Good protection, a dog like that.

MARTHA: That too.

OTTO: That dog's got to hate me.

MARTHA: Why?

OTTO: Cause I'm here now.

MARTHA: Yeah.

OTTO: Would like to get at my throat; I can tell.

MARTHA: I'll keep a watch that he doesn't hurt you.

OTTO: You think I'm afraid of the dog?

MARTHA: A dog is stronger than a man if he's big.

OTTO: He's fat.

MARTHA: All butcher dogs are fat.

OTTO: The fat ones ain't strong.

MARTHA: But they do it with their weight.

OTTO: Then I'd shoot him.

MARTHA: If you had a gun.

OTTO: Course I have one.

MARTHA: Where?

OTTO: At home, where it belongs.

MARTHA: All the things you have.

OTTO: Small caliber, but it's got a lot of zip.

MARTHA: At the slaughter house they have this detonator you can shoot an elephant with.

OTTO: Don't need to shoot no elephant.

MARTHA: But what if one attacks you?

OTTO: No way.

MARTHA: What if one breaks out of a circus? That's possible.

OTTO: You've got nothing but animals on your mind. That's all.

MARTHA: Was just an example. I've got an imagination.

# Scene III

(MARTHA *and* OTTO *are lying on the couch and making love. It takes some time before they speak.*)

OTTO: I don't feel no more love since you've been going with a dog.

MARTHA: That's a lie.

OTTO: That's what you say.

MARTHA: I know 'cause I was there.

OTTO: The way he licks under your skirt when you turn around. That made an impression on me right away the first time.

MARTHA: Every dog does that.

OTTO: He does that 'cause he wants something.

MARTHA: He doesn't want nothing. Don't worry about that.

OTTO: Hush. (*They make love more heatedly.*)

MARTHA: Ouch. Now you're hurting me.

OTTO: (*after it is over*) 'Cause that was an orgasm. (*brief pause*) But the last one you're going to get from me.

MARTHA: Anyone can say that afterwards.

OTTO: I stick to what I say. *(pause)*

MARTHA: There's no way of knowing what's on your mind.

OTTO: 'Cause you don't understand anything.

MARTHA: Why don't you explain what I don't understand.

OTTO: Don't know nothing about men. That's your mistake.

MARTHA: I'll learn how if you give me a little time.

OTTO: Can't learn that. You're born with it. *(pause)*

MARTHA: All you ever do is put me down.

OTTO: 'Cause I mean well. Otherwise, I wouldn't take the trouble. You're gonna see that I'm right.

MARTHA: I'm not saying nothing. But I need my time to get used to it; you've got to leave me my time.

OTTO: As long as you got the dog—no way.

MARTHA: Why, if I may ask?

OTTO: 'Cause he distracts you, which makes sense.

MARTHA: He certainly doesn't distract me; I wouldn't know how.

OTTO: And what with you having been a couple!

MARTHA: He's a liar who says that.

OTTO: You're pigheaded when it's time to confess. I've seen through everything; you can confess. 'Cause I knew it from the beginning. D'you think I'm blind? The way he slinks around you and licks you where he's got no business licking. And the way he hates me, the dog.

MARTHA: But you can't prove nothing. *(pause)*

You don't believe nothing I say; that's your mistake. I'm getting up now.

OTTO: Sure, now that it's over. (MARTHA *stands up and puts her butcher's coat back on.*)

You're an open book.

MARTHA: 'Cause you don't believe anything I say.

OTTO: Let's drop the subject; it's crystal clear. *(He turns to the side.)*

MARTHA: You going to sleep now?

OTTO: For half an hour, I'm tired.

MARTHA: Then I'm going to put the plant into a new pot; what I was going to do before.

OTTO: You've got a green thumb. That's for sure.

MARTHA: *(prepares everything on the table for the replanting operation)* 'Cause I have a secret. The soil I use I get from the meadow behind the church. That's better than the kind you buy.

OTTO: It's stolen.

MARTHA: If you take a close look at the meadow, you'll see the holes; they're mine. You're the only one I tell.

OTTO: That's stealing, that is.

MARTHA: Who'd object to my taking a little soil? *(big pause)*

OTTO: You're abnormal 'cause you're alone and 'cause you are not pretty.

MARTHA: I'm not in as much demand as you are.

OTTO: 'Cause you're not pretty.

MARTHA: I don't claim that I'm pretty.

OTTO: No one would believe you, even if you did.

MARTHA: What do you like about me anyway?

OTTO: I've got pity on you.

MARTHA: Don't need no pity. Can't buy anything with it.

OTTO: Pity is better than nothing.

MARTHA: *(makes no reply)*

OTTO: *(sleeps)*


# Scene IV

*(* MARTHA *stands at the door to her shop.* OTTO *arrives on a motorcycle.)*


MARTHA: Hello, Otto.

OTTO: Lying in wait for me. *(gets down from his motorcycle)*

MARTHA: I can stand by my shop door. It's not my fault if you pass by.

OTTO: 'Cause I have to pass by it on my way home from work.

MARTHA: Could've taken another way too.

OTTO: To make a detour just for your sake; you'd like that.

MARTHA: When you pass by, I say "Hello, Otto," 'cause we know each other.

OTTO: Stop bugging me.

MARTHA: Won't have nothing to do with me no more, eh?—'cause of the dog.

OTTO: Why don't you announce it to the whole world.

MARTHA: I've got to say it out here, if you don't come in. There's been a new development which will interest you. *(pause)* The dog is dead; now you don't need to be jealous anymore.

OTTO: How come he's dead?

MARTHA: 'Cause I've killed him 'cause of my love for you.

OTTO: Didn't need to do that.

MARTHA: I liked doing that for you.

OTTO: What an idea of love you got.

MARTHA: Love is everything for me. Anyway, it's all over with the dog. I put him in the garbage dump; you can go look at him.

OTTO: How'd you kill him?

MARTHA: With a knife. Which I really stuck into him.

OTTO: Did it hurt him?

MARTHA: Not at all. He fell over and didn't even howl.

OTTO: You didn't need to do that.

MARTHA: I fight for what I love.

OTTO: You didn't need to do that now that I've got another.

MARTHA: Where?

OTTO: None of your business. *(brief pause)*

MARTHA: Now that the dog is dead 'cause of you, you can't just drop me.

OTTO: I didn't tell you to kill him.

MARTHA: Sure you said it.

OTTO: Don't have to take everything literally.

MARTHA: If the dog is gone, I thought, then there'll be nothing separating us no more.

OTTO: What an idea of love you've got; it's bordering on imagination.

MARTHA: Got to stick to me. That's what you promised.

OTTO:    Nothing I promised. Is even grounds for divorce, a dog.

MARTHA: Let the dead rest in peace. Need you.

OTTO:    Anyone who did it with a dog has no right to a person.

MARTHA: Didn't do it with a dog. *(pause)* Can't do without you.

OTTO:    Then I'll come tomorrow since the dog is dead.

MARTHA: But the shop's closed now.

OTTO:    Tomorrow.

MARTHA: I'll be waiting for you.

OTTO:    *(climbs on his motorcycle)*

MARTHA: Watch out that nothing happens to you.


# Scene V

*(MARTHA and OTTO are lying on the couch. The dog is howling.)*


OTTO:    I can hear a dog howling.

MARTHA: I don't hear nothing.

OTTO:    There's a dog howling.

MARTHA: You're hearing ghosts.

OTTO:    There's a dog howling for sure.

MARTHA: Stuff up your ears. Then nothing will howl.

OTTO:    There's a dog howling.

MARTHA: That's Rolfi's spirit, he wants to scare you.

OTTO:    A critter's got no spirit.

MARTHA: If you can hear him howling he must have one, cause he's dead.
         You afraid?

OTTO:    I'm never afraid.

MARTHA: Why are you shriveling up then?

OTTO:    *(sits up)*

MARTHA: Stay, you're slipping out.

OTTO:    *(gets up and walks toward the freezer room. He unlocks and opens the door. The dog comes out, wagging his tail.)* Poor critter. Locking him up in there. You're a pig. The way he must have been freezing. *(He opens the back door and lets the dog out into the garden.)* Outside with you, move around, that'll warm you up. *(to* MARTHA*)* You pig, you're a sadist. *(He starts to dress.)*

MARTHA: Ain't you coming back?

OTTO: You spoilt my pleasure.

MARTHA: Better to freeze than to be dead, I thought. But he didn't understand what was at stake, stupid bastard.

OTTO: I'd have found out anyway that you lied to me.

MARTHA: I just couldn't do it.

OTTO: I told you: it's either me or the dog.

MARTHA: What if I just couldn't do it?

OTTO: But in the freezer you put him. You're really cruel. How cold you think it is in there?

MARTHA: Did it because of you.

OTTO: I said they should shoot him with that detonator at the slaughter house. 'Cause he's all played out and got to be punished.

MARTHA: Can do nothing right for you.

OTTO: 'Cause you do everything wrong.

MARTHA: But I don't mean to; 'cause I don't want to lose you.

OTTO: Who gives a shit.

MARTHA: What should I do now?

OTTO: With the dog between us there is no real love; it's only physical. 'Cause you're a pig, and that's obvious.

MARTHA: Let Him cast the first stone, says the Lord.

OTTO: No he doesn't.

MARTHA: Sure he says so.

OTTO: A Catholic but otherwise a pig.

MARTHA: Now, on top of the fact I didn't kill him I'm also getting insulted. That's what you get for being kind.

OTTO: 'Cause you got no feelings. Otherwise you'd know what the score is.

MARTHA: Precisely.

OTTO: Yeah. Then I'll bring my rifle tomorrow. You can kill him; otherwise it's over with us.

MARTHA: You can't force me.

*Farmyard & Other Plays*

OTTO:    I won't force you. You've got to want to do it. *(pause)* That'll be the killer.

## Scene VI

*(OTTO has brought his rifle.)*

OTTO:    Here's the rifle I told you I'd bring.

MARTHA:  *(takes it)* A real gun.

OTTO:    My property—now don't stand there but call him, and when he licks you shoot him between the eyes. Then it's all over. *(pause)* Now you can prove whether you've got guts or not.

MARTHA:  Promises have to be kept.

OTTO:    Yeah.

MARTHA:  *(walks to the window)* He's busy with his bone just now; let him finish eating.

OTTO:    Death isn't as hard on an empty stomach, everyone knows that. *(pause)* What are you waiting for?

MARTHA:  It'd be easier from the distance.

OTTO:    No way you'll hit him.

MARTHA:  Why don't you shoot, then.

OTTO:    That's your business. *(pause)* Forget about it if you don't do it now.

MARTHA:  You've got no patience with nothing.

OTTO:    'Cause you're stalling.

MARTHA:  *(takes another look out the window)* Now he's finished and doesn't have an empty stomach no more.

OTTO:    So you've been dawdling all this time to have an excuse. *(pause)* You better obey.

MARTHA:  I won't go up to him, that's for sure.

OTTO:    You've got to have a steady hand to hit him and got to shoot more than once. Otherwise it won't work.

MARTHA:  Now?

OTTO:    I won't talk no more; I've had my say.

MARTHA:  *(shouts out the window)* Rolfi, come here, look what Martha's got for you. *(aims)* He's coming. *(empties the entire clip)* I hit him.

OTTO:     *(goes to the window)* But he's still twitching.

MARTHA:  That's nothing. It's like with the chickens when you cut off their heads, and then they fly once more with their ghost.

OTTO:     Now it's all over.

MARTHA:  Right, dead he is, that's what I said.

OTTO:     Sure, you're a butcher.

MARTHA:  And I'm a good shot to boot.

OTTO:     You shot good, right. Now I'm going outside and put him in the garbage bin so that he's gone.

MARTHA:  I'd like to bury him.

OTTO:     First I throw him into the garbage bin. If you want, you can bury him later. Once you're dead you don't notice where you are.

MARTHA:  I can still bury him, the pick-up is only next week.

OTTO:     Right. *(OTTO goes outside)*

MARTHA:  *(at the window, speaking to OTTO)* So that's over and done with.

OTTO:     *(from outside)* He's heavy, the critter.

MARTHA:  Now I've got you; that's better.

OTTO:     *(comes back inside)* He's gone.

MARTHA:  Wash your hands.

OTTO:     We're sure being finicky. *(washes his hands)*

MARTHA:  Now everything is going to be different.

OTTO:     Sure. Got a beer? *(takes a piss)*

MARTHA:  Now don't start drinking again. You were plastered last night.

OTTO:     It having been Friday and my not having to work today gives me the right.

MARTHA:  But I still have to confess something 'cause of yesterday.

OTTO:     What did you do?

MARTHA:  You didn't notice.

OTTO:     What?

MARTHA:  Something slipped out of you in bed last night. You peed on me!

OTTO:     You pig. That's a lie.

MARTHA:  You can look at the sheet once we're home, 'cause I left it on the bed. A spot, like that.

OTTO:  I'll take a look at whose spot that is.

MARTHA:  You peed on me, but I won't hold it against you.

OTTO:  You pig!

# Scene VII

*(OTTO is lying on the couch, drinking beer out of a bottle. MARTHA is cleaning up the shop.)*

OTTO:  *(puts the empty bottle on the floor beside him)* Got another beer?

MARTHA:  At home, I had them bring a whole case for you.

OTTO:  I want it now.

MARTHA:  There is no more if you finished all three.

OTTO:  *(points to the empty bottles)* Two. Can't you count?

MARTHA:  Then there must be one more in the shopping bag, 'cause I bought three.

OTTO:  *(takes the third bottle out of the bag)* Sure. *(drinks) (pause)*

MARTHA:  Coming home with me?

OTTO:  I said I couldn't today, so I can't.

MARTHA:  I know why you can't. *(pause)*

OTTO:  I took pity on you, so stop bugging me.

MARTHA:  Don't want you spending time with someone else.

OTTO:  No one asked you. I'm hard as nails. *(pause)*

MARTHA:  You said everything would go my way; that's what you said.

OTTO:  Because of the dog, I thought I'd show her the real thing. I owe that to myself. Now show some gratitude and be patient.

MARTHA:  I am a human being too. *(pause)*

OTTO:  I need my freedom. I'll fight tooth and nail. You can't get enough.

MARTHA:  So I can't get enough.

OTTO:  Isn't normal to be so horny. *(pause)*

MARTHA:  It's easy to be fine and upstanding if it doesn't cost you anything.

OTTO:     I'm not fine.

MARTHA:   But a bastard.

OTTO:     Be glad you had at least one lover.

MARTHA:   I've got gratitude. *(pause)* You've got to learn to respect me, then everything will be different, I know that. Love needs proof.

OTTO:     'Cause you understand something about love. *(pause)*

MARTHA:   I am a business woman you can't simply kick around. My independence is worth something too. *(pause)*

          Everything would be all right with us, you said.

OTTO:     So you tasted blood. So what. *(pause)*

MARTHA:   You didn't pee on the other one.

OTTO:     If you talk about it once more I'll beat you to a pulp, and you'll never see me again. You keep saying that out of spite.

MARTHA:   But it's true.

OTTO:     It's up to you.

MARTHA:   I forgive you, and a new love begins.

OTTO:     Sure.

MARTHA:   Will you come home when I'm finished here?

OTTO:     You're pigheaded.

MARTHA:   I bought a filet of veal. It'll go bad if we don't eat it.

OTTO:     You've got a fridge.

MARTHA:   Filet of veal doesn't last long even in a fridge. *(pause)*

OTTO:     Either here and now or not at all. I won't go with you 'cause I've got plans.

MARTHA:   You've got no right to have plans.

OTTO:     'Cause you're cuckoo. Either here or not at all.

MARTHA:   All right then let's do it here if I can't change your mind.

OTTO:     I stick to my word. Next time perhaps I have more time. *(pause)* Take off your clothes. Just your panties, that's enough.

MARTHA:   That's better than nothing. *(They lie down together; after some time. . . .)*

OTTO:     *(straightens up)* It's not my fault if there is nothing doing with you.

MARTHA:   And it's not my fault if my body don't say nothing.

*Farmyard & Other Plays*

OTTO: 'Cause you've got no feeling.

MARTHA: Not true, but I'm difficult. I always said that.

OTTO: One goes to all that effort for your sake, and then there's nothing.

MARTHA: Don't do it intentionally. Got to give me time too.

OTTO: That sure takes long, giving you your time.

MARTHA: You're impatient with everything.

OTTO: I won't hold back just for your sake, or let's forget about the whole thing.

MARTHA: I didn't say a word.

OTTO: But think it. *(pause)*

MARTHA: I didn't think nothing. You don't have to give up the ship just 'cause it doesn't work one time.

OTTO: Not just once; happens often.

MARTHA: You're cross because I don't respond.

OTTO: 'Cause you got no humility, there is nothing doing. The dog was better, that's what you think; he knew how.

MARTHA: No.

OTTO: You've got no feeling 'cause you can't forget the dog.

MARTHA: Certainly not, now that I have you.

OTTO: That's what I thought too, that that would do the trick. The dog must have had something going for him. A critter, but on the ball.

MARTHA: That was different.

OTTO: From behind because a dog can only do it from behind.

MARTHA: No.

OTTO: I won't do that 'cause that's not for me.

MARTHA: That's all lies and not true. *(pause)* But we knew each other, the dog and I. There was an understanding.

OTTO: Then he licked. They like licking with their tongue, the dogs!

MARTHA: No!

OTTO: I don't lick. That's women's work.

MARTHA: Why?

OTTO: Because that is usual and a pleasure for the man. But you don't understand anything about men.

MARTHA: I never did that.

OTTO:    Trying is better than nothing. Everybody has to begin some-
         time.

MARTHA:  How?

OTTO:    Kneel down between my feet when I sit like this.

MARTHA:  *(does so)*

OTTO:    But I'll slap you if you bite.

MARTHA:  I'd never do that.

OTTO:    First like this, then all the way. Now try it.


# Scene VIII

*(OTTO is lying in his underpants on the couch.* MARTHA *has put on her butcher's coat.)*


OTTO:    That it doesn't give you the willies to wear the dirty coat on
         your naked skin.

MARTHA:  Doesn't give me no willies. *(pause)*

OTTO:    What are you doing?

MARTHA:  Nothing.

OTTO:    Then I'll get dressed.

MARTHA:  You want to go?

OTTO:    A man comes and then he leaves again. *(gets dressed)* By the
         way, where's the rifle I gave you?

MARTHA:  I put it in the closet 'cause you forgot it.

OTTO:    I'll take it along.

MARTHA:  Why?

OTTO:    Because it's mine, and that's why I'm taking it along.

MARTHA:  If you take the gun, you'll never come back.

OTTO:    You'd know.

MARTHA:  Sure.

OTTO:    Where's my rifle?

MARTHA:  *(takes the rifle out of the closet; looks at it)*

OTTO:    Put it on the table.

MARTHA: Let me hold it.

OTTO: What d'you want with a rifle, may I ask?

MARTHA: Want to look at it.

OTTO: That's nothing to look at. Hand it over.

MARTHA: Let me look.

OTTO: That's my property, and none of your business.

MARTHA: A gun always belongs to the one who holds it.

OTTO: You're a pig if you don't hand it over.

MARTHA: *(hesitates)* Let me have it as a memory.

OTTO: You're crazy. You've tasted blood, and now you ain't satisfied.

MARTHA: You led me on to the path.

OTTO: Then there has to be gratitude and not a shot.

MARTHA: But I get no pleasure.

OTTO: 'Cause you got no humility, there's nothing doing.

MARTHA: And you are saying that, you who peed on me, and I who forgave you.

OTTO: It's not my fault we don't make it.

MARTHA: Now I'm left in the lurch.

OTTO: 'Cause you ain't submissive, that's why.

MARTHA: But it's not that I mean to.

OTTO: But you ain't. Perhaps because the dog was better than I. An animal has no inhibitions; with him everything is possible.

MARTHA: You'd know not having been there.

OTTO: Everybody knows that. *(pause)* You're too sensitive, that's it.

MARTHA: All I want is for you to stay.

OTTO: People leave and they come back.

MARTHA: But the other one who's got your heart; you didn't pee on her.

OTTO: You're starting up again; there, you see.

MARTHA: All right, you didn't.

OTTO: I wasn't drunk then.

MARTHA: But with me, you can do anything when you're with me. *(pause)*

OTTO: I didn't know that we wouldn't make it.

MARTHA: You've got no respect at all for me, that's it. *(She shoots at* OTTO*; the shot misses.)*

OTTO: Stop, you pig, you almost hit me.

MARTHA: I meant to miss.

OTTO: But almost. Now give me the rifle or you'll get silly ideas.

MARTHA: Are you afraid?

OTTO: I'm never afraid.

MARTHA: And I can't make you afraid; that's it, even though I shoot better than you do.

OTTO: You can say that again, what with my love of guns.

MARTHA: Then we'll make a match. Trying is better than nothing. I'll start 'cause I'm the woman. *(aims and shoots Otto in the shoulder)* Bull's-eye, now it's your turn.

OTTO: I need a doctor. You wounded me.

MARTHA: First you've got to shoot.

OTTO: All right, I'll shoot if you want me to.

MARTHA: *(gives him the rifle)* Go ahead, shoot; I'm standing here. *(back to the spot where she was)*
*(stands completely upright)* Now you see that I'm not a coward; now you see what I'm like.

OTTO: You've got guts. *(shoots and hits)*

MARTHA: Bull's-eye.

OTTO: Sure.

MARTHA: Now it's my turn again.

OTTO: *(gives her the rifle, returns to his place)*

MARTHA: *(aims and shoots)*

OTTO: Bad luck 'cause your hand ain't steady no more.

MARTHA: Then it's your turn again or can I do it over?

OTTO: You can do it over 'cause you're a woman.

MARTHA: *(aims and shoots)*

OTTO: All good things come in threes. Try again.

MARTHA: *(shoots and hits)* Bull's-eye.

OTTO: Now it's my turn again. You hit me; there's a limit to everything.

MARTHA: Go get the gun; I don't feel well.

OTTO: Can't stand the sight of blood?

MARTHA: Why shouldn't I?

OTTO: Want to give up?

MARTHA: Certainly not, 'cause we just started.

OTTO: *(hesitates)*

MARTHA: Come get the gun. Got no guts?

OTTO: *(gets the rifle)*. You've got no idea what I can take.

MARTHA: But you've got to keep your distance like before. It doesn't count from close up.

OTTO: I'll go as far back as the wall. *(does so)*

MARTHA: Not necessary for you to go back that far.

OTTO: So that you can see what I can do.

MARTHA: Shoot. I'm standing here.

OTTO: *(aims, shoots, and hits)*

MARTHA: Bull's-eye, where is the gun?

OTTO: There's no rush; I won't run away. *(brings her the rifle)* I'm going back to my place.

MARTHA: Right, there've got to be rules. *(shoots and hits)*

OTTO: *(tumbles back toward the wall)*

MARTHA: *(puts the rifle on the floor, shoves it toward him with her foot)* There it is.

OTTO: Thanks. *(Aims, shoots, hits;* MARTHA *falls down face forward and remains lying there rigidly.)* (OTTO *looks at her, comes closer.)*
You give up?


CURTAIN

# A Man, A Dictionary

## A COMEDY IN THREE ACTS

*English Version by*
*Michael Roloff & Carl Weber*

## Characters:

MARTHA, a professional butcher, roughly forty years old.
OTTO, a worker, also roughly forty years old.
ROLFI, a German shepherd.

Otto is working on a machine. Martha has a shop. To make Martha's
work overly explicit or to suppress Otto's work in the *mise-en-scène* or
direction would not be good for the play.

*(A Man, A Dictionary* . . . is the new version of *Men's Business.* My
reason: what is the purpose of the continuous and futile representation
of the war between the sexes when things actually look different and
better in reality. So many people stick together come hell and high
water for a whole lifetime and often longer, while we others can
scarcely believe it.)

# ACT I

## Scene I

*(In the side room. After the shop has closed and in winter. Outside, in the garden, the dog is barking.)*

OTTO: This sure is a ceremony.

MARTHA: You are supposed to enjoy it when you are with me. So, I don't hold anything back. That's caviar—costs $1.30 the little jar.

OTTO: Caviar; tastes like fish.

MARTHA: Fish eggs is what it is.

OTTO: Tiny eggs.

MARTHA: He lays millions of eggs like that, the fish does. Got to put butter on it. That really brings out the taste.

OTTO: Like royalty.

MARTHA: That's nothing. You can't really do things up in the shop. When you come to my place, your eyes will pop at what I can really put out.

OTTO: *(eats)* But this ain't Russian caviar.

MARTHA: No.

OTTO: Yeah.

MARTHA: Domestic, what else. *(brief pause)* Why don't you stick to salami if you don't like it.

OTTO: Tastes okay. But Russian is better.

MARTHA: Did you ever eat real Russian?

OTTO: Everybody knows that. *(brief pause)*

MARTHA: I like it. *(brief pause)*

OTTO: Eating is good for you. *(pause) (They eat.)*

MARTHA: I'd go to the movies if you weren't here.

OTTO: What's playing?

MARTHA: *Gone With the Wind.*

OTTO: *(nods)* The novel.

MARTHA: An old movie I saw ten years ago. Unforgettable. You ever see it?

OTTO: No.

MARTHA: Want to go?

OTTO: So it's going to get real late? *(He denies her request.)*

MARTHA: You know the story?

OTTO: How can I if I haven't seen it.

MARTHA: I have.

OTTO: You can't know everything.

MARTHA: Shall I tell it to you?

OTTO: I'll buy the book and read it.

MARTHA: *(nods) (pause)* Say if you don't want no more. Then I'll clear the table.

OTTO: Sure. Clear it.

MARTHA: You don't want no more?

OTTO: Breakfast like a king, lunch like a businessman, supper like a bum—and you reach a ripe old age.

MARTHA: *(looks at him, nods)* Then I'll clear the table. *(does so)* *(while clearing)* I'm starting something new.

OTTO: What?

MARTHA: You've got three guesses.

OTTO: Don't want to.

MARTHA: 'Cause you couldn't anyway.

OTTO: Who cares?

MARTHA: *(laughs, finishes clearing the table, sits down again.)* *(A diary. She takes it out of her handbag.)* See? You can read what I've written.

OTTO: So what are you writing?

MARTHA: Go ahead, read it.

OTTO: Fiction.

MARTHA: No. Not when I'm serious. I wrote about you.

OTTO: What'd you write about me?

MARTHA: That you have entered my life is what I wrote. Go ahead, read it. It's true.

OTTO: *(reads)* Right.

MARTHA: There, you see what I'm like. You can read everything I've written. I've no secrets from you. *(laughs)*

OTTO:     I catch on to everything. *(goes on reading)*

MARTHA:   *(watches him)* What's beautiful in life you've got to hold dear. Then you've got something to remember when you have to. *(laughs) (watches him while he reads)* You like it?

OTTO:     I was never much good at "composition."

MARTHA:   I was. Because I've got imagination.

OTTO:     Me too. But the kind you can't write down. *(puts the book away)* The things I've thought of, you wouldn't believe me if I told you.

MARTHA:   What?

OTTO:     Perhaps I'll tell you sometime. Not now.

MARTHA:   Have it your way. *(takes the diary, takes a pencil from the cupboard, and starts writing)*

OTTO:     *(looks at her)*

MARTHA:   Be done in a sec.

OTTO:     Go ahead, if you want.

MARTHA:   So I won't forget it. *(She naturally writes "for him.") (pause)*

OTTO:     Everyone does what he likes. *(brief pause)* (OTTO *gets up and takes a magazine out of his briefcase.)*

MARTHA:   Whatcha got there?

OTTO:     Nothing; men's business.
          *(goes to the sofa, lies down and leafs through the magazine.)*

MARTHA:   *(stops writing)* Nothing but naked chicks. *(goes to him)*

OTTO:     It's not for you; men's business.

MARTHA:   *(sits down beside him.)*

OTTO:     Go on writing.

MARTHA:   I want to see what's in there. *(They look at the photos.)*
          I like that one best.

OTTO:     Average. There are better ones.

MARTHA:   Are they hookers, to let their pictures be taken like that?

OTTO:     You've got no idea what they are. *(brief pause)* Photo models; they ain't got nothing to do with hookers. Most of them go to college, and 'cause they can't pay for college they let their pictures be taken. Then they got money again and can live for another year.

MARTHA: So that's what they are like.

OTTO: Precisely, 'cause I know that.

MARTHA: And what do they earn when they get their pictures taken like that?

OTTO: Five thousand or more. *(brief pause)*

MARTHA: I wouldn't do that. *(brief pause)* Not even for five thousand.

OTTO: No one would pay you five thousand to take your picture. Take a look at how they're stacked.

MARTHA: *(leafs through the magazine)* That one ain't pretty either.

OTTO: Still, there's a difference.

MARTHA: If I'd be made up like that, and with a wig, you wouldn't recognize me.

OTTO: I'd recognize you no matter what, I bet. *(brief pause)*

MARTHA: But I wouldn't let my picture be taken like that. Not even for ten thousand. You can believe that. Besides, there's no need to, 'cause I am not in a fix like them.

OTTO: You don't know about nothing.

MARTHA: But I've got an imagination.

OTTO: Sure, that's something.

MARTHA: You want me to read what I just wrote?

OTTO: Big deal.

MARTHA: I'm doing it only for you. Put the thing away and I'll read to you. *(pause)*

OTTO: That's real love!

MARTHA: Sure.

OTTO: *(smiles; puts the magazine away)*

MARTHA: *(takes it and puts it back in* OTTO'S *briefcase)* That's where it belongs.

OTTO: *(smiles)*

MARTHA: *(goes back to the table, sits down, laughs)*

OTTO: I'm going to fall asleep if you don't read now.

MARTHA: *(reads)* February 1. Otto was here for the first time for dinner. We had cold cuts and caviar. Otto complained that it wasn't Russian caviar, but only domestic.

OTTO: Right.

MARTHA: If that's what you want. *(She begins to undress.)*
Aren't you going to take your things off?

OTTO: A man doesn't always have to take his clothes off. *(scratching and howling can be heard from the back door.)*
The dog wants to come in now.

MARTHA: But I won't allow it.

OTTO: Just what I expected, that he'd be acting up now. Pig. *(He gets up.)* Where's the leash?

MARTHA: Where it belongs.

OTTO: Filthy pig. *(He takes the leash and goes outside. One can hear him beat the dog; the dog stops howling and barks furiously.)*

MARTHA: There's more: I didn't even know that my Otto was such a gourmet. The next time I serve cold cuts, I am also going to buy Russian caviar, if it isn't too expensive. Still, he ate a lot, and he liked it. Now we are going to have a nice evening.

OTTO: You note down every little thing. *(He obviously likes this.)* What bullshit.

MARTHA: Tomorrow morning I am going to write down what else we did tonight. Just hints, but I'll understand. *(puts the notebook and the pencil away)*

OTTO: Now come here. That's better.

MARTHA: The dog is part of me, but you can beat it if you want to. Besides, he's been barking at people all day long, and the neighbors been cussing. He has it coming.

OTTO: *(from the outside)* You filthy dog, shut up now. *(The dog growls viciously.)*

MARTHA: He gets impatient 'cause he is not used to being outside such a long time.

OTTO: *(outside)* Scram, you pig. *(The dog attacks.)*

MARTHA: He's fond of me, he is.

OTTO: *(having difficulties)* How dare you attack me, you dirty pig. Watch out. *(One can hear OTTO and the dog fighting.)*

MARTHA: He doesn't like to be hit. He fights back then. *(She laughs to herself.)*

A Man, A Dictionary

OTTO: Filthy dog. Bastard. Hush, I said. Martha! Hush! He's going for my throat, Martha, you pig.

MARTHA: *runs to the door, tears it open, screams.)* Hush, Rolfi, Back to your spot!

OTTO: *(Comes back into the room in the meantime)*

MARTHA: And not another sound out of you, otherwise Martha will come and let you have it. And then all hell is going to break loose. *(The dog quiets down,* MARTHA *comes back inside.)*

OTTO: He jumped and wanted to bite me, the pig.

MARTHA: If a stranger hits him, he stands up to him.

OTTO: Precisely.

MARTHA: A dog knows at once whether somebody's got guts or is afraid.

OTTO: I ain't afraid. A pig is what the dog is. Sneaks between your legs, I've seen it.

MARTHA: He's jealous. That's normal.

OTTO: Yeah, a dog like no other.

MARTHA: I'm cold.

OTTO: Then come here. *(They both lie down on the sofa.)* *(pause)*

MARTHA: What's the matter?

OTTO: The dog's got to go. *(pause)*

# Scene II

*(MARTHA in her butcher's coat. OTTO is smoking, on the sofa.)*

MARTHA: *(works in the shop)* With a tripe shop you're always in business.

OTTO: Meat wherever you look.

MARTHA: You don't know what it is.

OTTO: Who cares.

MARTHA: If you knew about it, you could work for me. Need some help anyway.

OTTO: Do you think I'd stand around here all day long selling dog food?

MARTHA: I'd buy you a van and let you do the buying. A few hours in the morning at the slaughter house and you could spend the rest of the day in the sun. When you go to the market yourself, you've got better choice than when they just deliver, the way they do to me. But you've got to know your business. 'Cause buying is what can ruin you, or not.

OTTO: What do you pay?

MARTHA: We'd share everything.

OTTO: I'm earning more now.

MARTHA: How much?

OTTO: Eight hundred at least.

MARTHA: Gross?

OTTO: Net is what I write down.

MARTHA: I've got more.

OTTO: How much?

MARTHA: Twelve hundred in summer; in winter I sometimes get close to fifteen hundred.

OTTO: You're lying.

MARTHA: You can look at last year's books.

OTTO: What do I need your books for?

MARTHA: Have a look.

OTTO: Doesn't matter.

MARTHA: Besides, I'm independent, and you're not.

OTTO: Don't need no independence. Can't buy anything with it.

MARTHA: 'Cause you don't know it. Or you'd talk different.

OTTO: No one fucks with me at the shop, or else. You better believe me. Our gang is the best they've got. And they know it.

MARTHA: I'm not saying anything.

OTTO: Then you've got to shut up. I once had the highest piece-rate in a month. That was in July. Two years ago. I got a premium then. Thirty-four dollars.

MARTHA: Great.

OTTO: But only once. Now I can't make it anymore. I don't know why. I'm one of the best, but somebody else always gets the premium. Bad luck.

MARTHA: I wouldn't kill myself for thirty-four bucks.

OTTO: 'Cause you don't really count in your shop.

MARTHA: For myself I do.

OTTO: You don't think I do? Every movement I make at the packing machine is registered and counted at the end.

MARTHA: I like my business better.

OTTO: It's disgusting. No one should be allowed to make that much selling dog food.

MARTHA: Don't sell only dog food. But everything that has to do with innards. I learned my business and made my master butcher certificate 'cause I took over the business. My father even catered to a circus.

OTTO: For the tigers. That's impressive.

MARTHA: But now where there are no more little circuses, there is nothing doing. Big ones wouldn't bother with me; they think in bigger quantities.

OTTO: You ain't even got a schnitzel.

MARTHA: Schnitzel isn't innards. What nonsense. A tripe shop sells innards, nothing else. You've got to know that, and my customers know that too.

OTTO: So you aren't a real butcher.

MARTHA: No, 'cause I am specialized. Dad already did that 'cause he recognized a corner in the market. I could change over to a standard butcher shop any time I want to; the set-up is all there. But there are lots of butchers, and not many people left who know what to do with tripe. *(pause)* That's how it is.

OTTO: Anyhow, a woman as a butcher; that's unnatural. No matter how you look at it.

MARTHA: My parents had the shop, and I was their only child; just grew into it, and I was good at it. Being a butcher isn't an easy profession, and it requires a lot of love and ability. I accomplished it all, and as a woman.

OTTO: I'd rather be a man; there is no comparing that.

MARTHA: If I were a man, I would probably do even better. But the way things stand, my parents would say that I did all right. Turnover is constantly increasing. The mortgage I took when I renovated is almost paid back. I've got no other worries.

OTTO: Except you ain't got a man. Despite everything.

MARTHA: Believe me, I've had my chances. With everybody who comes in here day-in, day-out, but I've got my price too.

OTTO: And where did you drop your virginity? If I may ask?

MARTHA: That's so long ago that I can't even remember.

OTTO: Just as well at your age.

MARTHA: Right. *(a pause)* When you're in the shop from morning til night, that takes it out of you. *(laughs)* That doesn't leave you with much of a social life.

OTTO: Precisely. Nothing but dead critters all around you; no way to get any bright ideas.

MARTHA: Nobody knocks my business. That's my pride. A woman on her own doesn't have it easy. Everyone says so.

OTTO: You've got your dog.

MARTHA: We've always had a dog. As long as I can remember.

OTTO: Good protection, a dog like that.

MARTHA: That too.

OTTO: That dog really hates me.

MARTHA: *(laughs)*

OTTO: 'Cause I'm here now.

MARTHA: Sure, he isn't used to it.

OTTO: Would like to get at my throat; I can tell.

MARTHA: I'll keep a watch that he doesn't hurt you.

OTTO: You think I'm afraid of the dog?

MARTHA: A dog is stronger than a man if he's big.

OTTO: He's fat.

MARTHA: All butcher dogs are fat.

OTTO: The fat ones ain't strong.

MARTHA: But they do it with their weight.

OTTO: Then I'd shoot him.

MARTHA: If you had a gun.

OTTO: Course I have one.

MARTHA: Where?

OTTO: At home, where it belongs.

MARTHA: All the things you have.

OTTO: Small caliber, but it's got a lot of zip.

MARTHA: At the slaughter house they have this detonator you can shoot an elephant with.

OTTO: Don't need to shoot no elephant.

MARTHA: But what if one attacks you?

OTTO: No way.

MARTHA: What if one breaks out of a circus. That's possible.

OTTO: You've got nothing but animals on your mind. That's all.

MARTHA: Was just an example. I've got an imagination.

OTTO: You're too much alone. That's what it is. That has nothing to do with imagination.

MARTHA: That's why I have you now.


(MARTHA *and* OTTO *are making love.*)


OTTO: I don't feel no more love since you've been going with a dog.

MARTHA: That's a lie.

OTTO: That's what you say.

MARTHA: I know 'cause I was there.

OTTO: The way he licks under your skirt when you turn around. That made an impression on me right away the first time.

MARTHA: Every dog does that.

OTTO: He does that 'cause he wants something.

MARTHA: He doesn't want nothing. Don't worry about that.

OTTO: Hush. *(They make love more heatedly.)*

MARTHA: Ouch. Now you're hurting me.

OTTO: *(After it is over)* 'Cause that was an orgasm. *(brief pause)* But the last one you're going to get from me.

MARTHA: Anyone can say that afterwards.

OTTO: I stick to what I say. *(pause)*

MARTHA: There's no way of knowing what's on your mind.

OTTO: 'Cause you don't understand anything.

MARTHA: Why don't you explain what I don't understand?

OTTO: Don't know nothing about men. That's your mistake.

MARTHA: I'll learn how if you give me a little time.

OTTO: Can't learn that. You're born with it. *(pause)*

MARTHA: All you ever do is put me down.

OTTO: 'Cause I mean well. Otherwise, I wouldn't take the trouble. You're gonna see that I'm right.

*Farmyard & Other Plays*

MARTHA: I'm not saying nothing. But I need my time to get used to it; you've got to leave me my time.

OTTO: As long as you got the dog—no way.

MARTHA: Why, if I may ask?

OTTO: 'Cause he distracts you, which makes sense.

MARTHA: He certainly doesn't distract me; I wouldn't know how.

OTTO: I can't live together with the dog. *(pause)* You're pigheaded when it's time to confess. I've seen through everything, you can confess. 'Cause I knew it from the beginning. D'you think I'm blind? The way he slinks around you and licks you where he's got no business licking. And the way he hates me, the dog.

MARTHA: 'Cause you're afraid of him.

OTTO: No.

MARTHA: You are.

OTTO: You don't believe anything I say, and treat me like I was a pig. That's all you can do.

MARTHA: I'm getting up now.

OTTO: Sure, 'cause it's over now.

MARTHA: *(gets up, dresses)*

OTTO: I've seen through you.

MARTHA: 'Cause you're stupid.

OTTO: All you going to do is nod.

MARTHA: There is nothing to nod about. *(pause)*

OTTO: Let's drop the subject; it's crystal clear. *(He turns to the side.)*

MARTHA: You going to sleep now?

OTTO: For half an hour; I'm tired.

MARTHA: Then I'm going to put the plant into a new pot; what I was going to do before.

OTTO: You've got a green thumb. That's for sure.

MARTHA: *(prepares everything on the table for the replanting operation)* 'Cause I have a secret. The soil I use I get from the meadow behind the church. That's better than the kind you buy.

OTTO: It's stolen.

MARTHA: If you take a close look at the meadow, you'll see the holes; they're mine. You're the only one I tell.

OTTO: That's stealing, that is.

MARTHA: Who'd object to my taking a little soil? *(big pause)*

A Man, A Dictionary

OTTO: You're abnormal 'cause you're alone and 'cause you ain't pretty.

MARTHA: I'm not in as much demand as you are.

OTTO: 'Cause you're not pretty. A woman is supposed to look like something. *(pause)* Otherwise there is nothing doing.

MARTHA: I don't claim that I look like much.

OTTO: No one would believe you did, even if you claimed it.

MARTHA: What do you like about me anyway?

OTTO: I've got pity on you.

MARTHA: Don't need no pity. Can't buy anything with it.

OTTO: Pity is better than nothing.

MARTHA: *(makes no reply)*

OTTO: *(sleeps)*

# ACT II

## Scene I

*(*MARTHA *stands at the door to her shop.* OTTO *arrives on a motorcycle.)*

MARTHA: Hello, Otto.

OTTO: Lying in wait for me. *(gets down from his motorcycle)*

MARTHA: I can stand by my shop door and look out for customers. It's not my fault if you pass by and I say "Hello, Otto," like decent persons that know each other.

OTTO: 'Cause I have to pass by it on my way home from work.

MARTHA: Could've taken another way too.

OTTO: To make a detour just for your sake, you'd like that.

MARTHA: When you pass by, I say "Hello, Otto," 'cause we know each other.

OTTO: Stop bothering me.

MARTHA: Won't have nothing to do with me no more, eh?—'cause of the dog.

OTTO: Why don't you announce it to the whole world.

MARTHA: I've got to say it out here if you don't come in. There's been a new development which will interest you. *(pause)* The dog is dead; now you don't need to be jealous anymore.

OTTO: How come he's dead?

MARTHA: 'Cause I've killed him 'cause of my love for you.

OTTO: Didn't need to do that.

MARTHA: I liked doing that for you.

OTTO: What an idea of love you got.

MARTHA: Love is everything for me. Anyway, it's all over with the dog. I put him in the garbage dump; you can go look at him.

OTTO: How'd you kill him?

MARTHA: With a knife. Which I really stuck into him.

A Man, A Dictionary

OTTO: Did it hurt him?

MARTHA: Not at all. He fell over and didn't even howl.

OTTO: You didn't need to do that.

MARTHA: I fight for what I love.

OTTO: You didn't need to do that now that I've got another.

MARTHA: Where?

OTTO: None of your business. That's personal.

MARTHA: Now that the dog is dead 'cause of you, you can't just drop me.

OTTO: I didn't tell you to kill him. That's not my way.

MARTHA: Sure you said it.

OTTO: Don't have to take everything literally.

MARTHA: If the dog is gone, I thought, then there'll be nothing separating us no more.

OTTO: What an idea of love you've got. It's almost crazy.

MARTHA: Got to stick to me. That's what you promised.

OTTO: Nothing I promised. Is even grounds for divorce, a dog.

MARTHA: Let the dead rest in peace. Need you.

OTTO: Anyone who did it with a dog has no right to a person.

MARTHA: I never did it with a dog.

OTTO: But you thought of it.

MARTHA: Thought of it. What bullshit.

OTTO: No bullshit.

MARTHA: Can't do without you.

OTTO: Then I'll come tomorrow when the dog is dead.

MARTHA: But the shop's closed now.

OTTO: Tomorrow then.

## Scene II

*(In* MARTHA'S *apartment. The atmosphere is comfortable; it is evening.)*

MARTHA: New Year's Eve will be over tomorrow, and we won't have had anything of it.

OTTO: Don't need no New Year's Eve.

MARTHA: You've got to see everything. Otherwise you've got nothing to talk about.

OTTO: And what did the tickets cost?

MARTHA: That's my secret; 'cause you're invited.

OTTO: *(reads)* "A night in the Tropics." That can't be cheap.

MARTHA: Doesn't matter. *(pause)* We'll see. I'm inviting you.

OTTO: If we go, then I'd pay. That's men's business.

MARTHA: If you insist.

OTTO: I'll pay; otherwise I won't go.

MARTHA: A real gentleman. *(pause)*

OTTO: One bagful of surprises after the other with this woman.

MARTHA: You've got to take New Year's Eve as it comes.

OTTO: Now the dog is dead. You've got no heart.

MARTHA: Sure, 'cause I've got a brain in my head.

OTTO: Ain't the dog dead?

MARTHA: I've put an ad in the paper: "Friendly dog needs friendly home." *(She laughs.)* What's gone is gone.

OTTO: That's a confession.

MARTHA: You got your way.

OTTO: It's better this way. A corpse brings bad luck.

MARTHA: Right. Now he's got a nice home and is alive.

OTTO: How much d'you have to pay?

MARTHA: That's my secret.

OTTO: A fortune.

MARTHA: It's my money.

OTTO: Sure.

MARTHA: *(has started to put on her costume while they have been talking)*

OTTO: A costume?

MARTHA: Of course, otherwise it's no fun.

OTTO: I won't put on a mask; doesn't suit me.

MARTHA: There is no harm in trying. Look at me.

OTTO: What's that?

MARTHA: Guess.

OTTO:       Not much to see yet.

MARTHA:   Give me time. *(She continues to costume herself with great pleasure.* OTTO *enjoys watching her.)*

Now you must recognize it.

OTTO:       *(nods, but doesn't know).*

MARTHA:   A flower girl; can't you see that on first glance? *(She completes her costume quite consistently. It has been designed with much love and imagination, and does not look cheap. At the end she puts a big basket with flowers on one of her arms.)* You see? Elisa Doolittle, *My Fair Lady.*

OTTO:       *(quickly)* And me?

MARTHA:   Professor Higgins; who else?

OTTO:       Very clever.

MARTHA:   That took a lot of thinking till I hit on it. There, you've just got to put it on. I prepared everything for you.

OTTO:       Clever, and I've never put on a disguise in my whole life.

MARTHA:   I'd like to know what you've got against disguises.

OTTO:       *(carefully, pleasurably puts on his beautiful suit, presumably tails, etc.)* And me who has never been to a ball.

MARTHA:   I've been. As a child, but that makes no difference. Just stick to me and nothing will happen to you.

OTTO:       You think I'm afraid? *(He finishes dressing.)*

MARTHA:   You see, it fits.

OTTO:       *(smiles, nods)* Yeah.

MARTHA:   *(looks at her* OTTO*)* We really make a pair.

## Scene III

*(*MARTHA *and* OTTO *are lying on the couch. The dog is howling.)*

OTTO:       I can hear a dog howling.

MARTHA:   I don't hear nothing.

OTTO:       There's a dog howling.

MARTHA:   You're hearing ghosts.

OTTO:       There's a dog howling for sure.

MARTHA:   Stuff up your ears. Then nothing will howl.

OTTO:     There's a dog howling.

MARTHA: That's Rolfi's spirit, he wants to scare you.

OTTO:     A critter's got no spirit.

MARTHA: If you can hear him howling he must have one, 'cause he's dead. You afraid?

OTTO:     I'm never afraid.

MARTHA: Why are you shriveling up then?

OTTO:     *(sits up)*

MARTHA: Stay, you're slipping out.

OTTO:     *(gets up and walks toward the freezer room. He unlocks and opens the door. The dog comes out, wagging his tail.)* Poor critter. Locking him up in there. You're a pig. The way he must have been freezing. *(He opens the back door and lets the dog out into the garden.)* Outside with you, move around, that'll warm you up. *(To MARTHA)* You pig, you're a sadist. *(He starts to dress.)*

MARTHA: Better to freeze than to be dead, I thought. But he didn't understand what was at stake, stupid bastard.

OTTO:     Nothing but lies. Whatever you say. You didn't put no ad in the paper.

MARTHA: Sure I did. Take a look. It's in print. Even put it in twice.

OTTO:     And how come the dog's in the freezer? Where he doesn't belong?

MARTHA: 'Cause nobody answered the ad.

OTTO:     There are no animal lovers left in the world.

MARTHA: So I put him into a kennel for two weeks. And now he's back. If I'd given him to the A.S.P.C.A. they'd have put him to sleep by now.

OTTO:     I told you: it's either the dog or me.

MARTHA: I just couldn't do it.

OTTO:     But in the freezer you put him. You're really cruel. How cold you think it is in there?

MARTHA: Did it because of you.

OTTO:     I said they should shoot him with that detonator at the slaughter house. 'Cause he's all played out and got to be punished.

MARTHA: Can do nothing right for you.

A Man, A Dictionary                                                               119

OTTO:     'Cause you do everything wrong.

MARTHA:   But I don't mean to; 'cause I don't want to lose you.

OTTO:     Who gives a shit. With the dog between us there is no real love; it's only physical.

MARTHA:   You're crazy, that's it.

OTTO:     'Cause you're a pig, and that's obvious.

MARTHA:   What's happened has happened. Let him cast the first stone, says the Lord.

OTTO:     No he doesn't.

MARTHA:   Sure he says so.

OTTO:     A Catholic but otherwise a pig.

MARTHA:   Now, on top of the fact I didn't kill him I'm also getting insulted. That's what you get for being kind.

OTTO:     All you have to do is admit it, and it's over.

MARTHA:   So what. You think just because you've got a filthy mind like a pig that I've got to be one? And because you're crazy, my poor dog who hasn't got a home has got to suffer? *(pause)* Then we've got to put him to sleep if you don't want it any different.

OTTO:     Poor dog. And he tried to bite me. I know that for sure.

MARTHA:   'Cause he didn't know you. He ain't biting you now; you see that he is lying in front of your feet and licking them?

OTTO:     Not anymore.

MARTHA:   Right. If you don't stop complaining; take 'em along, Rolfi, and do with him what you want.

OTTO:     You'd like that, wouldn't you? I should call the A.S.P.C.A. 'cause of, 'cause of cruelty to animals.

MARTHA:   And all 'cause of that fucking dog.

OTTO:     It's not about the dog anymore. 'Cause from now on he stands under my personal protection. And now the two of us are going into the garden and move around a little because that makes you warm. *(Master and dog are going into the garden.)*

MARTHA:   *(By herself)* Right!

# Scene IV

(OTTO *is lying on the couch, drinking beer out of a bottle.* ROLFI *is barking outside as usual.*)

OTTO: *(puts the empty bottle on the floor beside him)* Got another beer?

MARTHA: Upstairs. I had them bring a whole case for you.

OTTO: I want it now.

MARTHA: There is no more if you finished all three.

OTTO: *(points to the empty bottles)* Two. Can't you count?

MARTHA: Then there must be one more in the shopping bag, 'cause I bought three.

OTTO: *(takes the third bottle out of the bag)* Sure. *(drinks) (pause)*

MARTHA: Are you coming up when I am through here?

OTTO: Not every night.

MARTHA: 'Cause you want to go to another.

OTTO: And so what?

MARTHA: Got no business going to another.

OTTO: Now that I took pity on you, you should keep quiet and don't start a fuss.

MARTHA: You said everything would go my way; that's what you said.

OTTO: I need my freedom. I'll fight tooth and nail, if nothing else works. *(pause)* You can't get enough.

MARTHA: So I can't get enough.

OTTO: Isn't normal to be so horny.

MARTHA: 'Cause I love you; there is nothing wrong with that.

OTTO: Not today. Everything in its time. Be glad you had at least one lover. Not everybody does.

MARTHA: I've got gratitude. You've got to learn to respect me, then everything will be different, I know that. Love needs proof. *(pause)* I'm giving you everything I have.

OTTO: 'Cause that is something.

MARTHA: You can't get everything for nothing.

OTTO: You want me to go? Men are prepared to split at any time. Just give the word.

MARTHA: I am just stating the facts.

OTTO: Who paid for the ball in the end?

MARTHA: I was happy and said "Thank you."

OTTO: Fifty bucks.

MARTHA. Yes. *(long pause)*

OTTO: A man like me doesn't even need to discuss this sort of thing. *(pause)* You can do without when a woman comes on like that.

MARTHA: I'm not coming on. Love you.

OTTO: 'Cause you understand something about love. *(pause)*

MARTHA: I am a business woman you can't simply kick around. My independence is worth something too.

OTTO: Cut out this independence shit. Don't you think I know by now that the lady is rich, and that I'm nothing but an asshole?

MARTHA: I never said that.

OTTO: But think it. *(pause)*

MARTHA: Forgive me and a new love begins.

OTTO: No. *(pause)*

MARTHA: Will you come home when I'm finished here?

OTTO: You're pigheaded.

MARTHA: I bought a filet of veal. It'll go bad if we don't eat it.

OTTO: You've got a fridge.

MARTHA: Filet of veal doesn't last long even in a fridge. *(pause)*

OTTO: Either here and now or not at all. I won't go with you 'cause I've got plans.

MARTHA: You've got no right to have plans. What with me doing everything for you.

OTTO: 'Cause you're cuckoo. Either here or not at all.

MARTHA: All right then let's do it here if I can't change your mind.

OTTO: I stick to my word. Next time perhaps I have more time. *(pause)* What's the matter now?

MARTHA: At once. *(She wants to undress.)*

OTTO: Just your panties, that's enough.

MARTHA: *(stops, looks down along herself, looks at* OTTO, *long pause)*

OTTO: What is it?

MARTHA: *(drops her skirt again, quickly)* We don't need to today. I thought about it. You can go so you won't be late.

OTTO: Very considerate. Real class.

MARTHA: And you're a bastard.

OTTO: Good-bye. *(off)*

MARTHA: *(by herself)* Martha, she sure was right.

# ACT III

## Scene I

*(In* MARTHA'S *apartment.* OTTO *is lying in the bathtub.* MARTHA *is in the kitchen and is cooking.)*

OTTO:  Bring me a new set of underwear. So I can reach it.

MARTHA: *(doesn't hear him)* What?

OTTO:  You're supposed to bring me a fresh set of underwear, or are you sitting on your ears?

MARTHA: At once. *(She finishes a few things quickly in the kitchen, then she goes into the bedroom and takes* OTTO'S *underwear from the closet and brings it to him to the bathroom.)* Here, I'm putting it on the heater. Then it will be warm when you come out of the tub.

OTTO:  Right.

MARTHA: Should I scrub your back?

OTTO:  No need to.

MARTHA: If you've got something, you don't know how to appreciate it. Everybody knows that. You've got a bath and an apartment and someone who scrubs your back—and what d'you have at home?

OTTO:  I move around; I am a man.

MARTHA: 'Cause all you've got is a crash pad.

OTTO:  So what.

MARTHA: Haven't even got your own room.

OTTO:  What should I do with a room? Once I even tried to rent an apartment. Almost. But then I didn't take it, after all. Waste of money.

MARTHA: What bullshit. Every person needs an apartment.

OTTO:  Not me.

MARTHA: But you like sitting in my bathtub, don't you?

OTTO:  Can get out of it.

MARTHA: First you're going to wash yourself. Dirty old dog.

OTTO:     *(laughs)* You like me?

MARTHA:   You silly.

OTTO:     I used to have a real build. You should have seen me. 'Cause I did sports.

MARTHA:   Wouldn't hurt you nowadays either.

OTTO:     Wherever you look, no flab.

MARTHA:   And there? *(poking his stomach)*

OTTO:     Muscles.

MARTHA:   *(does so)* Fat.

OTTO:     Just the surface, you don't understand nothing.

MARTHA:   Want me to scrub your back now? I like doing it.

OTTO:     *(smiles)* Admiring the naked facts.

MARTHA:   'Cause I've got the hots for them.

OTTO:     Horny as a march-hare.

MARTHA:   *(washes his back)*

OTTO:     The Japanese or Chinese have saunas. That really hits the spot with a man if he's bathed like that. 'Cause they've got the right touch, those geishas.

MARTHA:   I'm no geisha.

OTTO:     No.

MARTHA:   Your back has got to be clean, that's the most important thing. Like this.

          *(She is finished.)* Now don't waste more time 'cause the food is almost ready.

OTTO:     There's no fresh towel in sight.

MARTHA:   I forgot that. *(She goes back into the bedroom and returns with two fresh bathtowels.)* There—I'm going to set the table.

OTTO:     What are we having?

MARTHA:   Surprise.


A Man, A Dictionary

# Scene II

*(In* MARTHA'S *apartment.* OTTO *and* MARTHA *on the couch. It is evening.)*

OTTO: I would rent out the store and live the soft life.

MARTHA: You can't live off that.

OTTO: Then I'd look for a part-time job somewhere. If I were in your place.

MARTHA: Give up my business and let myself be exploited by someone else? I'm no idiot.

OTTO: The way she talks. *(pause)* You got no feminine qualities at all.

MARTHA: 'Cause I got a brain.

OTTO: But no feminine charms.

MARTHA: Rather a brain in my head than feminine charms.

OTTO: And what do I look like, a man who has to say: the woman who's got my heart is an independent butcher and makes more than I do.

MARTHA: Be glad that I do. *(pause)*

OTTO: I don't feel comfortable going out with you. When I told my colleagues about it, they agreed with me. If at least you were pretty.

MARTHA: If I were pretty, I am sure, I would not be as independent as I am.

OTTO: But wanted.

MARTHA: Bullshit. You've got an inferiority complex, that's it.

OTTO: I ain't got no time to have inferiority complexes. Never.

MARTHA: I made you an offer. Come to me. I give you a thousand in cash. And if things go on like this, I'll give you fourteen hundred in cash.

OTTO: And get myself into a worse hole?

MARTHA: That's only because you don't like having a woman boss.

OTTO: That's abnormal. Everyone says so.

MARTHA: I can't bother about that. Besides, I love my business. That's it.

*Farmyard & Other Plays*

OTTO:      That's abnormal too.

MARTHA:  You'd talk a different tune if you worked for me.

OTTO:      Never. A man is as good as his word. *(very fast)* Once at night
          I thought how I'd be lying there with my eyes open somewhere
          and be dead. You look and don't see anything 'cause it's all
          dark as far as you can see.

MARTHA:  Yes.

OTTO:      That's what I figured out. All the things I think of would fill
          an ocean.

MARTHA:  *(remains silent)*

OTTO:      Why ain't you talking?

MARTHA:  Now I thought about what you said and I got all tired.

OTTO:      Asleep?

MARTHA:  No.

# Scene III

*(The small side room.* OTTO *and* MARTHA. *It is daytime.)*

MARTHA:  It's bright daylight. What if someone sees us.

OTTO:      Nobody will see.

MARTHA:  But I'm afraid.

OTTO:      Because you've got no guts.

MARTHA:  And what if a customer comes, and I have to go out, and they
          notice.

OTTO:      You could put yourself right in a jiffy. A few quick touches
          and all traces are gone.

MARTHA:  It won't work 'cause I can't do that.

OTTO:      So they notice. What's there to notice? They see that there is
          a man in the house whom the woman loves. No matter the
          cost.

MARTHA:  You want the customers to find out and avoid me like a freak.
          Like the whole quarter being as Catholic as it is, so that there
          is no mercy.

OTTO:      What does a woman need a man for if she is married to her
          business?

A Man, A Dictionary

MARTHA: I'm doing enough for you.

OTTO: You still've got to plunge into the maelstrom of life and realize you're no exception.

MARTHA: Why?

OTTO: You've got no humility. None at all.

MARTHA: Bullshit!

OTTO: Come here and blow me!

MARTHA: What's that?

OTTO: That's women's work and a pleasure for the man. Don't need to undress, don't need to get excited, nobody feels nothin' but me.

MARTHA: What?

OTTO: Give me a blowjob, or don't you know that?

MARTHA: I've never done that.

OTTO: Trying is better than nothing. Everybody has to start sometime.

MARTHA: *(pause)* I'll do as you say; nobody's around at this time anyhow.

OTTO: Right. You unzip me, take him out and—feeling. 'Cause I'd slap you if you bit.

MARTHA: I'd never do that. *(stands about indecisively)*

OTTO: Best thing, you kneel down between my feet when I sit like this.

MARTHA: *(kneels down as he told her to, but waits; looks up at Otto, who is waiting too) (pause)*

OTTO: Don't pretend to be tired!

MARTHA: I almost really forgot that!

OTTO: What?

MARTHA: I would really have forgotten. That I had to wrap the stuff ready for Mrs. Oberwalder who's coming at three and everything got to be just the way she ordered it.

OTTO: Got plenty of time.

MARTHA: No. I can't get it out of my head with her being an old customer and faithful. I can't concentrate on you at all that way. 'Cause I usually get the packages ready early in the morning and now it's noon. *(She walks off into the store.)*

*Farmyard & Other Plays*

OTTO:    *(by himself, looks, pauses, softly)* Excuses!


# Scene IV

(MARTHA *is washing dishes.* OTTO *is reading the paper.*)


MARTHA: You got to stick together, Otto, otherwise you don't get anywhere in the world!

(OTTO *is reading and doesn't say anything.*)

MARTHA: Ain't ya listening?

OTTO:    I'm reading.

MARTHA: It's always what you want.

       *(pause)*

       Don't believe anything I say. *(pause)* Always working against me. Why?

OTTO:    I do what I want to.

MARTHA: You're living and eating at my place.

OTTO:    I still got my own pad.

MARTHA: But you're always here.

OTTO:    I'll go if you want to.

MARTHA: Don't want that.

OTTO:    Generous.

MARTHA: Love's got many sides which a woman can't do without. I know that now. But you got to watch out, otherwise you're swept away before you know it.

OTTO:    'Cause I'm the man.

MARTHA: Nothing wrong with that.

OTTO:    I'm reading. *(a long, long pause)*

MARTHA: *(washing the dishes)* Did you read the last thing I wrote in the diary?

OTTO:    Uninteresting.

MARTHA: A poem. *(pause)* The first poem I wrote since I can remember. *(pause)* Want me to read it to you?

OTTO:     No need to.

MARTHA:   But I would like to read it to you.

OTTO:     I've got my paper.

MARTHA:   There is nothing in the paper about you. But my poem is about you.

OTTO:     You're just boasting, that's obvious, 'cause I wasn't good at composition.

MARTHA:   You haven't changed since I got to know you. *(pause)* A little, but that ain't enough. You've got to have good will. *(pause)* Want me to read to you? Now that I'm finished in the kitchen.

OTTO:     Right.

MARTHA:   Let's go into the living room 'cause that's more comfortable. *(They do so.) (gets the diary and opens it up)*

OTTO:     First you kept it in the shop.

MARTHA:   It goes where I go. You just haven't noticed.

OTTO:     Uninteresting.

MARTHA:   I'm reading.

          (OTTO *nods.*)

MARTHA:   I don't have a title yet; that's still coming. *(reads)*

What a night your shadow's sight

Here I stand and reach, I am so small

You got so much to teach.

Second Verse:

All flowers have their blossoms

And the animals have a heart.

But what do we have of each other?

I can't think of anything at all.

Third Verse:

Don't mind being your servant in joy and suffering.

But not just that, 'cause there is nothing to my day

If I must bawl to please you.

Last Verse:
Stay by my side when I am tired at night
'Cause the day is crumbling,
And don't trample on my seed. Watch out.

Finished.

OTTO: The ending makes no sense.
MARTHA: That's poetry.
OTTO: Still.
MARTHA: Want me to recite it over?
OTTO: Once is enough.

# Scene V

(MARTHA *under the sunlamp.* OTTO *next to her.*)

MARTHA: You'll see the difference that makes, the tan.
OTTO: And I'll go blind in the meantime.
MARTHA: Don't look into it, then you won't go blind.
    *(pause)*
OTTO: Now that you don't see nothing 'cause you got your eyes closed, it could be that I would sneak away. Forever and ever.
MARTHA: That's the risk I take.
    *(pause)*
OTTO: It's all over with the love between us?
MARTHA: No. *(pause)* But there's something in you; you destroy everything that I've built up for the two of us. I know that now.
OTTO: But I don't mean to.
MARTHA: But you do it.
OTTO: Nobody can jump out of his skin. *(pause)* The use of a sun lamp without sunglasses is prohibited.
MARTHA: But then my eyes won't be tanned but have white edges. And that's ugly.
    *(pause)*

OTTO:    This way it's bad for the eyes.

MARTHA:  Really want me to put on the glasses?

OTTO:    Yes, 'cause I can't bear watching this.

MARTHA:  But if I look awful 'cause I've edges, then you shouldn't bawl
me out.

OTTO:    No, 'cause your eyes are more important.

*(long pause)*

(MARTHA *feels for the glasses that are lying next to her and puts them
on.)*

*(pause)*

MARTHA:  Can you see me?

OTTO:    Not so good 'cause I can't look into the light.

*(pause)*


CURTAIN